Wicked Salem

Exploring Lingering Lore and Legends

SAM BALTRUSIS

Globe
Pequot

Guilford, Connecticut

Illustrations on pages 2 and 5 by Sam Baltrusis.

Globe
Pequot

An imprint of The Rowman & Littlefield Publishing Group, Inc.
4501 Forbes Blvd., Ste. 200
Lanham, MD 20706
www.rowman.com

Distributed by NATIONAL BOOK NETWORK

Maps by Melissa Baker © The Rowman & Littlefield Publishing Group, Inc.

British Library Cataloguing in Publication Information available

Library of Congress Cataloging-in-Publication Data available

ISBN 978-1-4930-3711-7 (paperback)
ISBN 978-1-4930-3712-4 (e-book)

∞™ The paper used in this publication meets the minimum requirements of American National Standard for Information Sciences—Permanence of Paper for Printed Library Materials, ANSI/NISO Z39.48-1992

Printed in the United States of America

Contents

CONTENTS

Foreword

"Years of attempting to hide and distort the true history of Salem has made the job of modern-day researchers and historians that much more difficult."
—Tim Weisberg, *Spooky Southcoast & Haunted Towns*

When someone mentions Salem, Massachusetts, to anyone, anywhere in the world, chances are the first thing they'll think of is the Salem witch trials.

Over two hundred people were accused of witchcraft in 1692 and 1693 and twenty executed. Not exactly the kind of thing you want to put on a T-shirt or a billboard.

In a way, though, Salem should be proud to at least be known for something. There are over nineteen thousand cities and towns in the United States, and so many lack any kind of true identity. Usually, they find one thing they could be known for and try to make it something they are known for. *Hey, we have a lot of dandelions that bloom around town! We can call ourselves "The Dandelion Capital of the World"!* Festivals, parades, and pageantry ensue.

But in actuality, they're just reaching for something, trying to author their own identity—while Salem had its identity thrust upon it.

Witches, yes. But witches are just a small portion of what Salem has become, believe it or not. The witch trials themselves were just a brief period over 325 years ago, and although it had a serious effect on all that came after it, it shouldn't have been culturally definitive. In fact, it's the kind of thing you bury in your past, something that is only talked about in whispers, a blemish on what you hope is an otherwise fine reputation for your city.

But the identity of Salem came instead from the fact that it didn't hide its blemish. Sure, it took the city of Salem itself a couple of hundred years to finally be willing to identify itself as the "Witch City," but I'm talking about the people of Salem. While they may not have been particularly proud of the wrongs that were committed against innocent people accused of something most heinous, they did embrace the notion that Salem should have been more tolerant. And that tolerance has come to define what the city is all about today.

Salem isn't just about witches. It's about it being OK if you are a witch. It's about being able to gather with like-minded people, and believe in what you want to believe, and practice what you want to practice. Whether it's religion, belief, sexual orientation, artistic philosophy—Salem is a place where it is all on the table, and chances are, there will be others just like you gathered around that table.

But the journey there wasn't without its moments of shame and its attempts to hide Salem's horrific, but brief, moment on the world stage.

As the witch history was hidden, so was almost anything else that would be considered taboo. Ghosts, shadowy figures in the night, mysterious lights in the sky—anything that would be thought of as remotely paranormal would be shoved violently back into the recesses of the collective consciousness, under the oppressive premise of we're not that place anymore.

Now, fast-forward to the present. Years of attempting to hide and distort the true history of Salem has made the job of modern-day researchers and historians that much more difficult. As people are now ready to embrace that history, it's like a societal version of archaeology: You need to dig deep, find all the small pieces, and then try to put it all together to decipher the larger picture. Nothing can be taken at face value because nothing is as it seems.

When I began working on the television show *Haunted Towns* as a researcher and producer, the premise of my job seemed simple. I just had to find towns around the United States where there was a high level of paranormal activity at multiple locations and where that activity seemed like it could be connected to one central mystery that the cast of the show could then explore and figure out for themselves.

But it was easier said than done. So many towns wanted to hide their paranormal history because it was usually tied to some shameful tragedy of the past. Nine times out of ten, that's exactly why the town was so haunted, because the spirits were trying to get their story told rather than ignored. I encountered misinformation, half-truths, and things that were just out-and-out false at every corner, all while trying to explain to show runners, production company heads, and network executives why a place could be so haunted.

I call it "The Liberty Valance Effect," named after the famous line from the movie *The Man Who Shot Liberty Valance.* Everyone thinks the mild-mannered lawyer played by Jimmy Stewart is the one who shot and killed the vile outlaw Liberty Valance, but in actuality, Stewart had long lived with the secret truth that it was the cantankerous gunslinger played by John Wayne who was the hero. As Stewart's character is laying out the entire real story for a newspaper editor, he finally asks if he's going to run the story the real way it happened. The editor says "no" and tells Stewart something that has become a motto of the paranormal world: "When the legend becomes fact, print the legend."

Those legends permeate places like Salem. And it makes a researcher's job that much harder to have to sift through them and find those little pieces of the truth, scattered throughout, and assemble them into the larger, truer picture.

When it came time to do that with the history and mystery of Salem for an episode of *Haunted Towns*, I knew the person to call was Sam Baltrusis. While he can and will certainly print the legend, he's also going to print the fact, and explain why one morphed into the other. He's not content with just regurgitating the same stories that are told over and over again. He has a drive to look into all of the cracks of history and make sure no pieces of truth got left behind over the years.

As more than three centuries of pop culture and tourism have muddied the waters of this seaside city's true history, it's easy to say that *Wicked Salem* is one particular thing, one particular story to be told and that we know all there is to know. But as the lingering voices featured in this book will show you in the ensuing pages, the most wicked thing about Salem is how much we thought we knew . . . and how much we had left behind.

—Tim Weisberg, *Spooky Southcoast* & *Haunted Towns*

WICKED SALEM

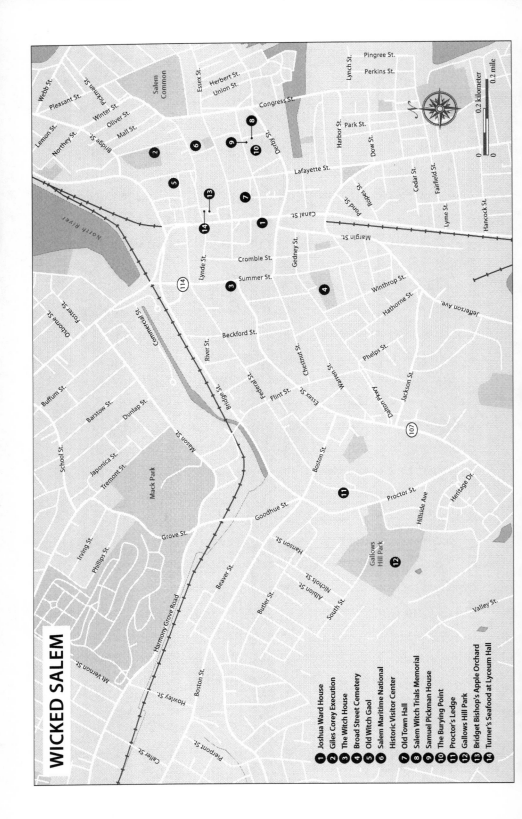

1. Joshua Ward House
2. Giles Corey Execution
3. The Witch House
4. Broad Street Cemetery
5. Old Witch Gaol
6. Salem Maritime National Historic Visitor Center
7. Old Town Hall
8. Salem Witch Trials Memorial
9. Samuel Pickman House
10. The Burying Point
11. Proctor's Ledge
12. Gallows Hill Park
13. Bridget Bishop's Apple Orchard
14. Turner's Seafood at Lyceum Hall

0.2 kilometer
0.2 mile

North River

Salem Common

Webb St.
Pleasant St.
Winter St.
Pickman St.
Oliver St.
Mall St.
Bridge St.
Northey St.
Lemon St.

Herbert St.
Essex St.
Union St.
Congress St.
Derby St.
Lafayette St.

Lynch St.
Pingree St.
Perkins St.
Harbor St.
Park St.
Dow St.
Cedar St.
Fairfield St.
Hancock St.
Lyme St.
Rogers St.
Pond St.

Canal St.
Margin St.
Jefferson Ave.

Cromble St.
Summer St.
Gedney St.
Winthrop St.
Hathorne St.
Lynde St.

Beckford St.
River St.
Chestnut St.
Phelps St.
Warren St.
Jackson St.
Dalton Pkwy

Bridge St.
Federal St.
Flint St.
Essex St.

Foster St.
Osborne St.
Commercial St.
Mason St.
Boston St.

Buffum St.
Barstow St.
Dunlap St.
Japonica St.
Tremont St.
Mack Park
School St.

Irving St.
Phillips St.
Grove St.
Goodhue St.
Hanson St.
Proctor St.
Hillside Ave
Heritage Dr.
Gallows Hill Park

Harmony Grove Road
Beaver St.
Butler St.
Albion St.
Nichols St.
South St.
Valley St.

Mt. Vernon St.
Howley St.
Boston St.
Pierpont St.
Caller St.

114
107

Introduction

What is it about the sleepy New England city that engenders itself to history's witches, rakes, and rogues?

Salem, Massachusetts, suffers a bit of an identity disorder. There are two versions of the so-called Witch City that have symbiotically etched themselves into the collective unconscious: There's the iconic, blood-stained Salem that boasted a sadistic sorority of witch-hanging zealots in the late 1600s, and then there's the modern, witch-friendly spectacle that welcomes thousands of supporters into its coven of commercialism every October.

It's a tale of two Salems.

As far as the paranormal is concerned, the city is considered to be hallowed ground. However, based on my personal experience as a local historian and tour guide, Salem has a love-hate relationship with its ghosts. Why?

"The city has a long history of not wanting to get wrapped up in commercializing its witch history," explained Tim Weisberg, host of the radio show *Spooky Southcoast* and researcher with Destination America's *Haunted Towns*. "It's something they've only really embraced over the past couple of decades. There's still a bit of an 'old guard' in the city that doesn't want to see anyone capitalizing on witches, ghosts, or things of that nature."

WICKED TIMELINE

JANUARY 1692
In present-day Danvers, Elizabeth "Betty" Parris and Abigail Williams start to have fits in the Rev. Samuel Parris household in Salem Village.

JUNE 10, 1692
Bridget Bishop, sentenced to death by hanging on June 2, was executed. She was the first of twenty to be executed and the only victim to be hanged alone.

JULY 19, 1692
Sarah Good, Elizabeth Howe, Susannah Martin, Rebecca Nurse and Sarah Wildes were hanged.

AUGUST 19, 1692
Rev. George Burroughs, Martha Carrier, George Jacobs Sr., John Proctor and John Willard hanged.

SEPTEMBER 19, 1692
Giles Corey was pressed to death over a two to three-day period.

SEPTEMBER 22, 1692
The so-called "eight firebrands of hell" were hanged including Martha Corey, Mary Easty, Alice Parker, Mary Parker, Ann Pudeator, Wilmot Redd, Margaret Scott and Samuel Wardwell.

OCTOBER 12, 1692
Governor William Phips forbids imprisonment of anyone else of witchcraft and ends the Court of Oyer and Terminer ten days later.

MAY 1693
Governor Phips orders the release of the remaining accused witches upon payment of their prison fees.

As Salem's on-air expert for the national *Haunted Towns* TV show, I helped Weisberg hunt for locations with ties to the witch trials of 1692. It was tough. "As they've let some of that guard down and television shows have come in, it's been my experience that the 'powers that be' who control many of the allegedly haunted and historic locations have been disillusioned with the way productions have come in and treated its history," Weisberg told me. "At least, that's what I heard in the rejections I received from certain locations when attempting to get permission to film *Haunted Towns*."

Known for its annual Halloween "Haunted Happenings" gathering, it's no surprise that the historic Massachusetts seaport is considered to be one of New England's most haunted destinations. With city officials emphasizing its not-so-dark past, tourists from

PHOTO COURTESY OF FRANK C. GRACE

Author Nathaniel Hawthorne met his wife, Sophia Peabody Hawthorne, at a lavish dinner party at the Grimshawe House, 53 Charter Street, next to the Old Burying Point.

all over the world seem to focus on the wicked intrigue surrounding the 1692 witch trials.

Originally called Naumkeag, Salem means "peace." However, as its historical legacy dictates, the city was anything but peaceful during the late seventeenth century. In fact, when accused witch and landowner Giles Corey was pressed to death over a two-day period, he allegedly cursed the sheriff and the city. Over the years, his specter has allegedly been spotted preceding disasters in Salem, including the fire that destroyed most of the downtown area in June 1914. Based on my research, a majority of the hauntings conjured up in Salem over the city's tumultuous four-hundred-year-old history have ties to disaster, specifically the one-hundred-year-old fire that virtually annihilated the once prosperous North Shore seaport.

Cursed? Salem is full of secrets.

My first ghost tour experience in Salem was an impromptu trek on Mollie Stewart's "Spellbound" tour in 2010. I remember gazing up at the allegedly haunted Joshua Ward House and being convinced I had seen a spirit looking out of the second-floor window. It turned out to be a bust of George Washington. Soon after writing my first book, *Ghosts of Boston*, I signed on to give historical-based ghost tours of my own in a city that both excited and scared me. I let Salem's spirits guide me.

One of my first face-to-face encounters with a negative entity was at the Joshua Ward House. I felt a warm sensation on my chest one night in September 2012 while I was giving a ghost tour. It felt like a spider bite. However, I wasn't prepared for the bitter truth. After the tour, I lifted up my shirt and noticed three catlike scratch marks on my chest. In the paranormal world, this is called the

WICKED BY THE NUMBERS

OVER 150 ARRESTS, 54 CONFESSIONS, 28 CONVICTIONS,
19 HANGINGS, 5 DEATHS IN THE WITCH GAOLS AND
1 MAN, GILES COREY, PRESSED TO DEATH.

PERCENTAGE OF MEN AND WOMEN WHO WERE ACCUSED BUT INNOCENT OF WITCHCRAFT IN 1692.

EXECUTIONS IN 1692 INCLUDED 15 WOMEN,
5 MEN & 2 DOGS. 5 DIED IN THE DUNGEONS
INCLUDING SARAH GOOD'S INFANT CHILD.

TOWNS IN 1692
NUMBER OF INNOCENTS ACCUSED BY TOWN

WITCHCRAFT EXECUTIONS

CASUALTIES BY TOWN

SALEM: 10	MARBLEHEAD: 1
ANDOVER: 3	ROWLEY: 1
TOPSFIELD: 2	IPSWICH: 1
WELLS, ME: 1	AMESBURY: 1

"mark of untrinity" and it's said to signify the touch of a demonic entity. I was terrified.

After the incident, I refused to get too close to the haunted and potentially evil structure.

In 2015 the Joshua Ward House at 148 Washington Street was purchased by Lark Hotels and was transformed into a boutique hotel. Renamed "The Merchant," the posh overnight haunt celebrates Salem's rich maritime past. No mention of the reported ghosts and demonic entity allegedly lurking in the shadows of this chic new hot spot.

Are the new owners in complete denial of the structure's haunted history? Probably.

Listed on the National Register of Historic Places in 1978, the three-floor Federal-style building had a stint as the Washington Hotel in the late nineteenth century. It stood vacant for years and was restored in the late 1970s. When Carlson Realty moved into the his-

PHOTO COURTESY OF FRANK C. GRACE

The Joshua Ward House at 148 Washington Street in Salem was purchased by Lark Hotels and was transformed into a boutique hotel called "The Merchant" in 2015.

toric house, mysterious events started to occur. Chairs, lampshades, trash cans, and candlesticks would be found turned upside down when the staff arrived in the morning. Papers were strewn on the floor, and candles were bent in the shape of an S. One of the offices on the second floor is ice-cold, a telltale sign of paranormal activity.

Why would the Joshua Ward House be haunted?

The structure was built on the foundation of Sheriff George Corwin's old house, and many people believe the venerated sheriff's spirit lingers at the 148 Washington Street locale. In fact, after mysteriously dying from a heart attack at age thirty, his body was buried beneath the building but was later interred at the Broad Street Cemetery.

George Corwin was arguably the city's most despised man, and rightfully so. The then-twenty-something sheriff reportedly got a kick out of torturing the men and women accused of witchcraft. Although it was the uncle, Magistrate Jonathan Corwin, who tried and accused the innocents, it was the sick and twisted nephew who enforced the unjust verdicts.

"Sheriff Corwin was so disliked by the people of Salem, that when he died of a heart attack in 1696, his family didn't dare bury him in the cemetery for fear he'd be dug up and his body torn limb from limb," wrote Robert Ellis Cahill, himself a former Essex County sheriff turned author, in *Haunted Happenings*.

Corwin's cruelty is legendary. For example, he sent an officer to accused witch Mary Parker's home in Andover on September 23, 1692, literally the day after her execution, demanding that her son fork over the dead woman's farm and goods. Parker's son, who was still mourning the loss of his mother, had to cough up a large sum of money to stop Corwin's demands for corn, hay, and cattle.

WICKED WISDOM: LAURIE CABOT

"How do you undo two thousand years of propaganda?
There was so much false information and misinterpretation."
—Laurie Cabot, *Salem's Official Witch*

In most of the interviews that I conducted for *Wicked Salem*, one name kept coming up like a well-crafted spell whispered from the Witch City's collective lips.

Laurie Cabot.

The "Official Witch" of Salem, known for her outspoken and sometimes controversial approach, still has that all-knowing fire that magically emanates from the high priestess well into her twilight years.

Hex and the city? Laurie Cabot, the first lady of witchcraft, earned her magical legacy in modern-day Salem. PHOTO COURTESY OF JEAN RENARD

"She might be eighty-five but she's still going strong," said my friend Memie Watson when I asked about setting up an interview with her mentor. Watson, a high priestess who also teaches at Enchanted in Salem's Pickering Wharf, said Cabot is still wicked busy "writing books, teaching classes, and making her crafts and oils."

Then I got the call. Cabot agreed to meet with me. When I walked into her workshop, I was immediately overwhelmed by her positive energy. She radiates wisdom. It's all around her.

"I didn't plan on living in Salem," she told me about her move from Boston's North End to the Witch City in the late 1960s. "My purpose in life at the time was to teach witchcraft as a science. I had no idea anybody was going to notice me."

While I'm chatting with the grande dame of witchcraft, I'm amazed by the artifacts assembled behind her. There's a wall full of antique dolls—including a miniature version of Cabot—and stacks of books from all religious traditions. Her desk is covered with beads and objects that sparkle.

Think *Alice in Wonderland*. And I fell into Salem's rabbit hole.

"I didn't plan any of this," she said, adding that the universe has been her guiding force throughout most of her magical life. "It was all by accident. But I have to admit, I was naive at the time."

As the high priestess was speaking, I heard three loud knocks on the wall behind her. I looked up. Was it a ghost? "Oh, those are my fairy knockers," she said, checking with her daughter Penny to make sure the front door was locked. "They were sent over from Cornwall. It's usually a warning of some sort."

Apparently, Cabot gets a heads-up when there's danger nearby. In fact, she avoided an issue with carbon monoxide a few years ago thanks to her Cornish pixie friends. "The knockers saved my life," she insisted.

Unfazed by the phantom knocking incident, Cabot continued talking about her early days teaching a ten-session class on the science of witchcraft in Wellesley, followed by a stint at Salem State. Apparently, she was too "flamboyant" for the college circuit even though her classes were popular with the students.

"I dressed a bit more conservative back then," she said with a smile, pointing out her signature look that includes a black robe, two-tone hair, cat-eye makeup, a tattoo on her cheek, black-rimmed glasses, and a large pentacle hanging around her neck. "I'm much different now."

There's no doubt that Cabot's legacy continues to thrive in the North Shore's tight-knit Wiccan community. But what about Salem's coven of commercialism in October? It's her fault. Well, kinda sorta.

It actually started when Cabot's black-cat familiar, Molly Boo, climbed up a tree when she lived on Chestnut Street. "Molly Boo outed me," she said about the incident that catapulted her into international fame. Her cat climbed a tree outside of her apartment and got stuck about fifty feet up, and wouldn't come down for three days. Cabot contacted everyone, including the police. No one would help her. She feared that Molly Boo would die.

In desperation, Cabot called the local newspaper. "They were only interested in the story because I was a Witch," she recalled. "I told them that Molly Boo was my familiar and I wanted my cat out of the tree."

According to Cabot, a man came with a pole that had a loop and he quickly rescued Molly Boo. "One of the guys said, 'Don't put a curse on us,' and I just rolled my eyes," she said with a laugh. Of course, a local photographer captured the animal rescue, and the photo was picked up by hundreds of papers across the globe.

Soon after, Cabot opened Salem's first "witch shop" in 1970. Armed with her newfound notoriety, she wanted to dispel the myths and misconceptions related to modern-day witchcraft. However, she had no idea how difficult it would be to educate the public.

"How do you undo two thousand years of propaganda?" she emoted. "People used 'witch' as an umbrella term for magic in all cultures. There was so much false information and misinterpretation."

Witches, she explained in a *New York Times* article published in the 1970s, "don't sacrifice animals or people or drink blood or eat babies or any of that stuff."

When asked about the hysteria in Salem more than three centuries ago, Cabot said witchcraft has been associated with evil intentions and devil-worshipping for generations. "They couldn't find a witch in Salem in 1692 because they had no idea what they were looking for," she responded. "They had it all wrong."

Cabot did shy away from the history associated with the witch trials. However, she believes the Salem of today is the polar opposite of the Salem of 1692. "In many ways, I believe those innocent people gave their lives for us," she said, adding that the local Wiccan community honors the twenty victims from the Salem witch trials during Samhain, the Celtic feast of the dead.

For the record, she doesn't believe the victims of the witch trials were actually practicing pagans.

After being declared Salem's "Official Witch" by then-governor Michael Dukakis in 1977, Cabot's popularity flourished. She appeared on scores of television shows, including *Oprah*, and radio broadcasts and was featured in dozens of newspapers and magazines. Cabot even ran for mayor on a so-called witch's platform before publishing her book, *The Power of the Witch*, in the 1980s.

In an article published in the *Salem Evening News* on October 25, 1989, Cabot was dubbed the "first lady of witchcraft," and the piece also talked about how she made Salem the "witch capital of the world."

She even wrote an opinion piece for the *New York Times* that ran on October 31, 1989. "As a witch, I am appalled at the way society views us," she wrote. "On the one hand, we are portrayed as silly, green-skinned hags flying on broomsticks across children's Saturday cartoons. On the other, we are used as scapegoats for all the bizarre cult crimes and violent rituals staged by misguided individuals who think they are practicing witchcraft."

The op-ed was called "Witches, Without Warts."

While Cabot's fame skyrocketed, a backlash started to develop in the 1990s. Salem wanted to focus on its maritime history and totally forget that its past was soaked in blood. "Our witch history makes us special," she said. "Every single city up and down the coast has maritime history. They all have pirates and lighthouses. Salem's history was becoming polarized."

Yes, Salem can celebrate both witches and pirates.

In 1997 Cabot was involved in a minor courtroom drama and newspapers wanted to tarnish her reputation. "It was hard to tell who was real then," she said, obviously hurt by the backlash. What would she say to the people from the dark period in her life? "Do your research," she shot back. "Study what I've studied. Ignorance is bliss."

As Cabot talked about the painful episode from her past, the soundtrack from Disney's *Frozen* mysteriously started to play from a TV next to her workshop. The song? "Let It Go."

Now in her eighties, Cabot's fire has simmered a bit. However, she's still passionate about educating the masses. When asked about the witch-on-broom silhouettes that are still perpetuated in pop culture, she told me that it's demeaning. "If you are going to have witches fly on brooms, there's no reason to make us look horrific," she said, referring to Margaret Hamilton's green-skinned crone stereotype from the 1939 film *The Wizard of Oz*. "Either they portray us as horrific-looking with warts or supercilious," she added.

As far as the Spooky World–style shenanigans that have transmogrified Salem every October, Cabot isn't a fan. "I'm still not sure what a guy with an ax in his head and blood dripping down his face has to do with witchcraft," she told the *Boston Globe* in 2017. "Some of it is offensive. The fun house. The scary murderous stuff. It brings bad vibes. It's projecting the wrong kinds of things."

Cabot is also wary of the ghost hunters on TV who don't respect the dead. Witches, she explained to me, communicate with spirits during rituals by calling in their ancestors. As a high priestess, Cabot is able to cross between both worlds. She's able to invoke both the living and the dead. "Ghosts don't harm people," she said. "They don't scratch or sit on us."

She also talked about poltergeist phenomenon: It's a "quirk of energy from the living," she explained. In other words, people can manifest "thought forms" without even knowing they are doing it. "A poltergeist is not from another realm," she said. "It's not a ghost or spirit. It's something else."

As my interview with the grande dame of witchcraft was coming to an end, she asked me what I was calling the book. "*Wicked Salem: Exploring Lingering Lore and Legends*," I said. "Of course, you're the legend." Cabot's face lit up. "I like that," she said with a smile.

I then asked one more question before heading out. How does the first lady of witchcraft respond to people who blame her for Salem's commercialism? "I say thank you," Cabot mused. "And you're welcome."

Luckily, the "Myths & Misconceptions" tour I gave on weekends in 2016 focused more on history and less on Salem's ghosts. Oddly, many of the haunts from my past—including Essex Heritage's main office at 10 Federal Street—ended up on the tour. Yes, Essex Heritage's office had a past life as Salem's Old Witch Gaol.

The original dungeon in which the accused witches were held was constructed between 1683 and 1684. The subterranean jail was 70 by 280 feet and was made of hand-hewn oak timbers and siding. The conditions in the prison were notoriously horrific. Prisoners were held in small cells with no bedding. There were no bars on the cells, but if the prisoners ran away from their punishment, they were generally caught and immediately executed.

Prisoners were charged for straw bedding and food, and if they could not afford them, they did without. Water was also withheld from prisoners, since the Puritans believed they would be able to get more "confessions" if the prisoners were thirsty. The salaries of the sheriff, magistrate, and hangman were also paid by the prisoners, and they were billed for cuffs and other bonds and even for the tortuous acts of searching their bodies for "witchery marks" and getting their heads shaved in the process.

At least five died from the inhumane conditions in the dungeon. It's also notoriously haunted.

There's supposedly a prison guard–type apparition making his nightly rounds. His image has been caught on camera. Adam Page, an investigator with F.I.N.D. Paranormal, said he has proof there's an angry sentinel spirit guarding the former witch gaol site. "The old guard at 10 Federal Street is really angry," said Page, a former case manager with Paranormal Salem. "We always run into his full-bodied apparition at that building."

Page said that during his days working at Paranormal Salem, he would get a bad vibe from the Colonial-era sentinel. "The full-bodied apparition we caught at 10 Federal was walking straight down the hallway," Page explained. "He didn't see us, so I think he's more of a residual haunting. But he could be intelligent. If you looked in the door, he walked right to left."

I was happy to learn that the "Myths & Misconceptions" tour was based in the Salem Visitor Center on New Liberty Street and not the Old Witch Gaol location. And, yes, the old Salem Armory building is also allegedly haunted. However, it's more of a residual energy relating to a five-alarm fire that destroyed most of the structure on February 22, 1982.

PHOTO COURTESY OF FRANK C. GRACE

Opened in 1816 and used as headquarters for the city's government until 1837, Old Town Hall is known for its ghostly inhabitants wearing period garb.

On one of my tours, a woman from California flipped out when I spoke in front of Salem's Town Hall. The out-of-town visitor on my tour swore she saw two ghostly faces pressed against a window on the second floor of Town Hall, as if they were intently listening to what I said. I nodded when she told me. "Yep, I know the ghosts of Salem are listening," I said, followed by a nervous laugh. She had no clue what I've seen.

Nestled next to the highly trafficked Burying Point, which is also known as the Charter Street Cemetery, in Salem, the Samuel Pickman House is now owned by the Peabody Essex Museum. Tour groups pass this historic building, and passersby peek through its windows. Several people on my tours believe they've seen a full-bodied apparition of a girl peering from the upper-floor window. Others claim the small Colonial-era structure is

PHOTO COURTESY OF FRANK C. GRACE

The Samuel Pickman House, located on the corner of Charter and Liberty Streets, is said to be home to an evil entity connected to a horrific murder committed centuries ago.

home to a demonic entity that manifests in photos taken through the seventeenth-century building's old-school windows.

One ghastly story tells of a husband and wife who lived in the Samuel Pickman House with their seven-year-old daughter. Similar to the demonic infestation in Stephen King's *The Shining*, an evil entity is rumored to have caused the husband to go insane.

According to legend, the man chained his daughter up in the attic, torturing and starving the child. He then tied his wife to a tree outside and killed her by pouring hot wax over her body, leaving her to die a slow, painful death. The possessed man then fled, leaving the dead child in the attic and his murdered-by-wax wife tied to the tree.

People on my walking tours who have taken photos of the house claim it is still inhabited by a demonic force. There are many reports of the ghost of the young girl looking out the attic window at the crowds below.

After doing exhaustive historical research, I found no real proof to suggest that the story of the murder or the supposed demonic infestation at the house is true. However, the building is a surefire hot spot of photographic anomalies, ranging from orbs to a mist that envelops the structure.

Next to the Samuel Pickman House are the Witch Trials Memorial and the old cemetery. My most profound encounter in Salem was at the Burying Point on Charter Street several years ago. I spotted a full-bodied apparition of a lady in white coming from what I learned later was the gravestone of Giles Corey's second wife, Mary. It's my theory that Mary Corey's residual energy is looking for her husband. She's heading oddly toward the very spot at the present-day Howard Street Cemetery where the stubborn but determined old man was crushed to death. Yes, love does exist in the afterlife.

While historians have agreed that Corey was fatally pressed near the Old Salem Jail, they've been unsure about the execution site where nineteen innocent men and women were hanged for witchcraft in 1692.

Apparently, X does mark the spot, and it's located behind a Walgreens.

WICKED WISDOM: MARGO BURNS

"The more you know about a person,
the harder it is to demonize them."
—Margo Burns, *Records of the Salem Witch-Hunt*

When historian Margo Burns pitched the idea of a lecture examining the genesis of the rye-based ergot poisoning theory and its ties to the Salem witch trials, she jokingly called the topic "the fungus among us."

Yes, she's talking about Salem's moldy bread myth.

Compared to her more serious contemporaries specializing in the witch-trials hysteria, Burns approached the topic with humor. "If you haven't figured it out already, I'm a ham," she joked, sporting her trademark bowtie. "But I'm not a ham on rye." *Ba-dum-bump.*

Levity is Burns's secret weapon. And so is her lineage. She's a great-granddaughter eight generations down to witch-trials victim Rebecca Nurse.

After listening to her speak at a lecture organized by Salem's Witch House about the origins of the controversial ergot theory, Burns tackled a much larger issue associated with the witch trials of 1692. Pop culture continues to twist Salem's history—and Burns wants to untangle it.

Burns told me that her fascination with the witch trials was ignited during the summer of 1995 when she started to learn more about her famous ancestor. She recalled holding the original

Historian Margo Burns has been featured on TLC's *Who Do You Think You Are?* as Salem's witch-trials expert. PHOTO COURTESY OF MARGO BURNS

document written by the Reverend Samuel Parris indicting Nurse. It was a turning point for the linguistics scholar turned historian. "It was a bit strange to read a detailed description of my relative's genitalia," she said, explaining that the obvious scars related to childbirth and old age that was somehow interpreted as a so-called witch's teat in the trial document. "I don't think you have to be a descendant of a victim to truly understand the gravity."

What Burns learned from her initial research is that just because it's a primary source doesn't necessarily mean that it's fact. "You can't believe everything that it said or written, even if it's coming from a primary source," she said. "In some cases, you have to literally read between the lines."

Nurse, respected by her Salem Village community, was initially acquitted of witchcraft charges. However, her innocent verdict was reversed after the afflicted girls continued to have fits during the interrogation. Nurse was hanged at the gallows at Proctor's Ledge on July 19, 1692. Years after the execution, the verdict was deemed unjust by the Colonial government and ultimately reversed.

In Nurse's pretrial hearing, silence literally equaled death.

Burns told me that one explanation for her ancestor's ultimate demise was that Nurse was hard of hearing. When the magistrate asked the seventy-one-year-old woman a question, she failed to respond. "Apparently, the girls really started to flip out and the jury kept coming in and out. It was so noisy in the courtroom, she couldn't hear what was going on," Burns explained. "Because she was elderly, she probably didn't answer because she couldn't hear. If you were asked a question and you refused to answer it, that could be used against you. Silence was considered proof of guilt."

As the associate editor and project manager of the comprehensive book *Records of the Salem Witch-Hunt*, Burns is now armed with an arsenal of original witch-trials documents and is respected for her ability to debunk the myths perpetuated by the media and pop culture.

Her underlying motivation: How do we know what we know?

It was this basic question that inspired her to tackle Arthur Miller's *The Crucible* after watching the 1996 film adaptation starring Daniel Day-Lewis and Winona Ryder. Burns recalled being unnerved by the play-turned-movie's historical inaccuracies. In response, she crafted a comprehensive analysis of what Miller got wrong.

"It's a constant challenge because you have to untangle *The Crucible*," she said. "I'm all for creative license, but I wish he used different names."

In her online essay "Arthur Miller's *The Crucible*: Fact & Fiction," Burns skillfully lists the inaccuracies perpetuated by the Pulitzer Prize–winning playwright. For example, Abigail Williams was born in 1681 and didn't have a romantic relationship with the sixty-year-old John Proctor. Williams was eleven in 1692, and the alleged affair didn't happen because of the age difference. Proctor wasn't a farmer but rather a tavern owner. Even though Williams is portrayed as the niece of the Reverend Samuel Parris, we're not exactly sure how she was related to Parris. Also, the reverend's wife was alive during the witch trials. She had two children in addition to Betty Parris.

Burns believes Miller pulled some of the more outlandish myths from Charles Upham's *Salem Witchcraft*, first published in 1867.

For example, Tituba didn't lead some wild dance party in the woods. And, more importantly, she wasn't an African-American caricature perpetuated in the late 1800s. "Tituba wasn't a voodoo-practicing black mammy from Barbados. She was an Indian," Burns continued. "She got recast by how people saw the world during the Civil War."

According to Burns, every generation interprets history with a biased lens. "My era is the coercion of false confessions," she said. "I strongly believe they were planning to execute all of those who confessed. They were heavily trying to get people to confess because it was simply a lot easier to convict them."

The historian said the "how do we know what we know?" lens should be applied to Miller's take on the Salem witch trials.

"People see things in their periphery," she explained. "We fill in those gaps."

However, Burns said *The Crucible* playwright successfully tapped into the mythic, Joseph Campbell–style motif that "people you trust can turn on you," which resonates with contemporary audiences and continues to make the Salem witch trials so disconcerting. "People can be mean to each other to the point they could have someone killed," she said. "There are so many reasons that could ultimately result in mortal harm. Holding a grudge could result in people dying."

After spending a decade collaborating with Bernard Rosenthal on *Records of the Salem Witch-Hunt*, Burns redirected her lens to the controversial ergot poisoning theory.

Introduced by Linnda Caporael in the 1976 edition of *Science* magazine, the undergrad student turned professor noticed a link between the strange symptoms reported by Salem's afflicted girls and the hallucinogenic effects of drugs like LSD. Acid is a derivative of ergot, a fungus that affects rye grain. Mental effects of ergotism include mania, headaches, vomiting, and even psychosis. It also resulted in gangrene and it was common for victims to randomly lose body parts like fingers and ears.

The ergot poisoning theory has been slammed by scholars like Stephen Nissenbaum, historian and coauthor of *Salem Possessed*. He publicly disputed the moldy bread myth, saying that it "appears unlikely to me that this would not happen in any other year, in any other household and in any other village." However, people who visit Salem year after year still believe it's a viable explanation for the madness that unfolded in 1692.

"I was one of those people who wanted to dispute it," Burns told me. Of course, her initial impression changed after she did the unthinkable and contacted the original source of the ergot theory. Yes, she actually reached out to Linnda Caporael.

Burns said she was shocked to learn that the woman behind the controversial theory was oblivious to the backlash. "When I talked with her, she didn't know about Nissenbaum's response," Burns said. "Based on our conversation, she thought the negativity was directed toward Mary Matossian. That moment of the conversation gave me pause." For the record, Matossian cited Caporael's theory in the 1982 edition of *American Scientist,* in which she argued that the symptoms of Salem's afflicted resembled some of the hallucinatory effects associated with ergot poisoning.

According to Burns, Caporael was merely applying the scientific method in her original *Science* magazine article, while Matossian was absolute in her attempt to present ergot as a feasible possibility. Burns said Caporael's suggestion that there could have been a medical explanation for the witch-trials hysteria is conceivable using the scientific method. "It's interesting to me what people hear and how they extract information," Burns explained. "The scientific method is a completely different way of looking at the world."

During her presentation at the Witch House event, Burns raised a few eyebrows when she defended Caporael. However, the historian effectively weaved together a narrative giving a trippy and sometimes hilarious backstory to the counterculture-colored lens of the 1970s. Burns also presented a few of the sensational newspaper headlines associated with Caporael's article and then discussed the country's LSD-laced point of view a half century ago which culminated in Timothy Leary's "tune in, turn on, drop out" call to action.

When Burns decided to "take ergot head-on," she said it was important for her to go directly to the theory's originator. "Every story has a source. Who knows when it first started? It's rare to actually know the flashpoint," she said.

The idea that ergot poisoning was to blame for the Salem witch trials was simply a by-product of Caporael's time. "Linnda got it right," Burns mused. "Well, she got the scientific method right."

But how did Caporael's moldy bread myth impregnate pop culture? Burns cites the hundreds of newspaper articles with over-the-top headlines as the culprit. Apparently, it was a slow news day. "People have agendas regarding how they interpret the past," she continued. "We use facts to say what we want them to say."

Meanwhile, the featured expert from TLC's *Who Do You Think You Are?* is redirecting her focus to one of the more vilified characters from Salem's witch-trials past, William Stoughton. He was the chief justice overseeing the special court of Oyer and Terminer and was somehow overlooked when Arthur Miller assigned the title of "hanging judge" to John Hathorne in *The Crucible*.

When asked if she views Stoughton as the ultimate bad guy, Burns said she is trying her best to be objective. History shouldn't be interpreted with black-and-white thinking. "The more you know about a person," she said, "the harder it is to demonize them."

Salem earned international ink, once again, in early 2016 after a crew of experts supposedly pinpointed the exact location of the gallows. For the record, I wrote about the "Proctor's Ledge" location in 2013. "One piece of new evidence emerged from court notes dating back to August 1692," I wrote in my book *Ghosts of*

Salem. "Rebecca Eames, a woman suspected of witchcraft who was taken from her home in Boxford, said she saw the gallows from Boston Street while on her way to downtown Salem. The latest theory is that the true site is located behind the Walgreens located at 59 Boston Street."

It was this historical document from Eames that was used to identify the location of Gallows Hill. In July 2017 the city unveiled a memorial honoring the twenty victims of the Salem witch trials at the exact location of the executions.

As far as how they were executed, historians aren't sure if the hangings were on locust trees, which were probably not strong enough for an execution, or if the accused were hanged from traditional gallows. "Contemporary accounts make clear that the prisoners uttered their last words, with nooses around their necks, from ladders," wrote Frances Hill in *Hunting for Witches.* "When the ladder was pushed away from whatever it was leaning on, they died a slow, painful death. But whether the ladder was supported by a branch or a scaffold, the sources do not say."

There is also debate about the skeletal remains of the victims. "Bone fragments have been found," said a representative from the Peabody Essex Museum about an excavation at Gallows Hill Park, "but we'll never really know what they were from." At least three victims from 1692—Rebecca Nurse, George Jacobs Sr., and John Proctor—were brought back by relatives, salvaged in the wee hours of the night, and given a proper burial. The remains of the other seventeen victims, which have been the subject of rumors that they were exhumed and relocated by wealthy merchant Philip English and other theories claiming they were buried beneath the cellar of a church in nearby Marblehead, are believed to be dumped in either a ditch or within the rocky crevices of Proctor's Ledge.

Kathryn Rutkowski, visitor services manager with Essex Heritage and creator of the "Myths & Misconceptions" tour, brought me to the granite bench honoring the first victim executed in Salem during the 1692 witch-trials hysteria. Her name? Bridget Bishop.

Bishop lived in Salem Village (present-day Danvers) but owned property on the eastern side of Salem's current Washington and Church Streets. As far as witchcraft, several men accused her of dabbling in the dark arts. John Cook Jr., an eighteen-year-old who lived on Essex Street, just opposite First Church, claimed he was awakened one morning by Bishop's specter, which was grinning at him. She "struck me on the side of the head, which did hurt me very

The city dedicated a new memorial at Proctor's Ledge, the spot where historians believe that nineteen innocent men and women were hanged for witchcraft in 1692.

much," he claimed. Bishop allegedly returned and caused an apple to fly from Cook's hand into his mother's lap.

Cook's neighbor, Samuel Shattuck, testified that Bishop's lacy garb was un-Christian, and when she visited the Shattuck home, their son began crying and became "stupefied and devoid of reason."

Born Bridget Playfer, Bishop was originally married to Samuel Wasselbee and had two children. Her entire family, husband and children, died under mysterious circumstances. In 1664 she married Thomas Oliver and had a daughter, Christian. Oliver also died, and Bridget remarried to Edward Bishop, hence her namesake.

Yes, the woman had a checkered past.

She was known as a penny pincher, and a local Salem woman claimed in 1682 that Bishop's specter, with Alice Parker, who was also accused and executed as a witch, pulled her down to the beach and tried to drown her. Of course, this was ten years before the trials and a precursor to the accusations that would ultimately lead to her demise on June 10, 1692.

Historically, Bishop is credited with running a scandalous tavern near the present-day Lyceum. However, it's more likely that she's been confused over time with Sarah and Edward Bishop, who ran a watering hole out of their home down the street. They were sent to Boston's less-strict jail and managed to escape.

Bridget Bishop wasn't so lucky.

My first paranormal experience in Salem involved Bishop. Soon after I wrote *Ghosts of Boston*, I signed on to give historical-based ghost tours of my own in a city that both excited and terrified me. I let Salem's spirits guide me. I had several odd experiences outside of Lyceum Hall, which was said to be Bridget Bishop's tavern. However,

PHOTO COURTESY OF FRANK C. GRACE

Bridget Bishop was the first person executed for witchcraft during the Salem witch trials of 1692.

it was her orchard. An apple mysteriously rolled out of nowhere in the alley behind what is now Turner's Seafood. I looked up. No one was there. I accepted it as a peace offering from Bishop.

My perceptions of Bishop have changed since my first encounter with what I believed to be her ghost in 2013.

Kathryn Rutkowski and I talked about the misconceptions associated with the only victim hanged alone. "Out of all of the executions, we know the most about Bridget," Rutkowski told me one day in early June, which was oddly the day before the anniversary of Bishop's murder. Rutkowski and I started tearing up when we talked about the crimes against humanity that unfolded in Salem in 1692. "They could have just put the noose around Bridget's neck and killed her instantly," she emoted. "But they didn't. The executioners actually positioned the noose so she would die a slow,

Mary Corey, the second wife of witch-trials victim Giles Corey, is buried in Salem's Old Burying Point.

horrible death. She was hanging in the gallows—convulsing and losing control of her bowels—in front of a crowd of people. They were publicly shaming her before they killed her."

As we talked, I fought to hold back the tears. I had the ultimate realization. I was standing in the middle of New England's deepest, darkest secret: Salem's soil is still soaked with blood, and its ghosts have unfinished business.

I. The Witches

PHOTO COURTESY OF FRANK C. GRACE

During the witch-trials hysteria, the John Ward House was literally across the street from the dungeon and is reportedly haunted by tortured spirits from Salem's 1692 past.

WITCH HAUNTS

1. Bridget Bishop's Apple Orchard
2. Bridget Bishop House (Location)
3. The Rebecca Nurse Homestead
4. Pressing of Giles Corey
5. Cinema Salem, Alice Parker
6. Ann Pudeator's House
7. Susannah Martin's Home
8. Ingersoll Ordinary
9. Alice Parker's Home
10. Redd's Pond
11. Wimott Redd Memorial
12. Peirce Farm at Witch Hill
13. Easty Property
14. John Proctor House
15. Parris Foundation
16. St Peter's Episcopal Church
17. Salem Witch Trials Memorial
18. Salem Meetinghouse
19. Bewitched Sculpture
20. John Ward House
21. Parson Barnard House
22. Elizabeth Howe Mural
23. Proctor's Ledge
24. Solart-Woodward House

Alice Parker

When I appeared on Destination America's *Haunted Towns* in 2017, my goal was to give a voice to the victims of the Salem witch trials and to focus on stories that may have been overlooked by history. One piece of testimony from 1692 involving a "spectral hog" has always creeped me out.

Yes, it's about a ghost pig.

Scott Porter and Brannon Smith from *Haunted Towns* interviewed me near Giles Corey's granite marker in Salem's Witch Trials Memorial in early April 2017. As soon as I started to speak on camera, it mysteriously started to snow.

"Cinema Salem was the location for one of the taverns," I explained on *Haunted Towns*. "And taverns were a hotbed of activity in Salem at the time. In fact, that's where innocent people were brought in for pretrial examinations. The victims were stripped down naked and searched for witch marks."

Alice Parker, one of three victims from what is present-day Salem, had a husband who was a local fisherman who frequented both of the Beadle taverns. One night she marched into the Samuel Beadle tavern to scold her husband for spending too much time in the pub. When her husband's drinking buddy, John Westgate, tried to intervene, Parker called Westgate a "rogue."

"There is something that happened outside of that tavern and people are blown away by this," I said on national TV. "There was a spectral pig sighting outside of that tavern and it was used to accuse and execute a woman, Alice Parker."

"Oh wow, a spectral pig?" Porter asked me. "Yes, it was a ghost pig," I responded, having no idea my comment would go viral online.

Westgate testified that on his walk home he and his dog were pursued by a "spectral pig"—a figure with the body of a hog but the face of accused witch Parker.

"Here's what really happened," I continued. "John Westgate was in the bar with Alice Parker's husband. She came in to get her husband because he was out drinking, staying out a little too late. John Westgate said he saw Parker outside of the tavern. She had the shape of a hog and her face was on the pig. Spectral evidence was just made-up stuff, like saying 'I saw a ghost pig,' and they used it as evidence to accuse and execute her."

In Salem, taverns were the epicenter of the 1692 witch-trials hysteria. Examinations of hundreds of innocents accused of witch-craft were held at local watering holes like Ingersoll's Ordinary in Danvers and Thomas Beadle's tavern located at 65 Essex Street. For the record, the Parker and Westgate incident happened at the other drinking spot, Samuel Beadle's tavern. Several of the accused who were eventually executed—including Parker, Ann Pudeator, and the Reverend George Burroughs—had their pretrial hearings at the Salem tavern on Essex Street, and in the case of Burroughs, they were locked in a room for days before their inquest.

"The pretrial hearings of George Jacobs Sr. and his grand-daughter Margaret were held at Beadle's," explained the official guide to the Salem witch trials tercentenary. "Margaret confessed under duress from the authorities and in doing so helped to convict her grandfather and George Burroughs, former minister of Salem Village. She later recanted her confession, but the men were hanged anyway. Margaret herself escaped probable execution only because she was too ill to stand trial."

There was also the now-famous "ghost pig" sighting outside the second tavern owned by the Beadle family, located near the present-day site of Cinema Salem and St. Peter's Church. "During Alice Parker's hearing, one John Westgate testified that a black hog had attacked and nearly devoured him one night just across the street from Beadle's tavern," the witch trials tercentenary guide confirmed. "Because his faithful dog fled from the beast instead of attacking it, Westgate deduced that the hog was actually Alice Parker or another specter she had sent to hurt him."

Parker lived in a modest-size house near present-day 54-58 Derby Street that she and her fisherman husband rented from Mary English. Based on several accounts, Parker may have suffered from paralyzing fits of catalepsy. She also had a reputation for clairvoyance and on one occasion successfully predicted that a friend's husband had died at sea.

Catalepsy? Parker was found January 12, 1692, lying on a muddy bank near the present-day House of the Seven Gables. She looked as if she were dead. When she was carried to her home and placed on her bed, she suddenly came to, sat up, and laughed. It was these trancelike states that were used as evidence to execute her.

Witches were believed to leave their bodies as "specters," and these entities supposedly did their out-of-body dirty work.

Westgate used "spectral evidence" testimony against Parker. He recounted his journey after leaving Samuel Beadle's tavern. "Going from the house of Mr. Daniel King, when I came over against John Robinson's house, I heard a great noise . . . and there appeared a black hog running towards me with an open mouth, as if he would devour me," Westgate said in court.

Mary Warren, an afflicted girl who worked as John Proctor's maid, testified against Parker in May 1692. Warren said Parker bewitched her mother to death, made her sister sick, and drowned men at sea. Parker's response? "I know nothing of it," she protested, but the court cited more disasters. "I never spoke a word to her in my life," she continued.

Parker was brought to trial on September 9 and executed at Proctor's Ledge with seven other innocents on September 22, 1692.

ALICE PARKER'S HAUNT: CINEMA SALEM

Popcorn and ghost pigs? The city's only independent movie theater, Cinema Salem, is the last house standing in a neighborhood that formerly boasted seven entertainment venues.

Names like the Federal Theatre, the Empire, and the Comique thrived during the city's vaudeville era. The Plaza Theater, formerly located at 273 Essex Street, was built in 1913 and burned down four years later. Almost all of Salem's entertainment complexes closed during the Great Depression, but others, like the Paramount built during the 1930s, survived until 1971. It was torn down to make way for the Witch City Mall.

The current Cinema Salem in the indoor complex had a past life since the 1970s, ranging from a USA Cinema to a Loews in the 1980s to the Salem Flick. The three-screen theater reopened in 2006 as an art-house gem known as Cinema Salem.

According to assistant manager Peter Horne, the ghosts from its silver-screen past still linger. "Multiple coworkers have had experiences here in the theater," he said. "In the past, we've had psychics, ghost hunters, and paranormal investigators inside."

Horne said a former manager spotted what looked like a man in black sitting in theater No. 3 when he was upstairs in the projection booth. "He looked down and saw someone sitting in the theater," Horne recalled. "There was no movie playing, so he freaked out and ran down to kick them out. The man disappeared. According to him, he looked like a middle-aged man, wearing coat-tails. His clothing was from the Victorian era."

After giving a tour of the theater, Horne walked me up to the cramped projection area. "It's very uncomfortable in here at times," he said. "I'm not sure if it's because it's surrounded with concrete and it's just cold and dark, or if there is something else going on. Anybody who has been up in the projection booth says it's creepy and uncomfortable to be up here."

There are other reports of the mystery man's reflection in the projection booth's window. Also, smoke has mysteriously emerged from the corner spot in theater No. 3, believed be the favorite seat of the ghostly man wearing Victorian-era garb. Perhaps he smoked a pipe?

One former manager said she felt an unseen force push her while leaving the projection booth. "She said multiple times that she felt a force pushing her down the stairs, almost kicking her out," Horne claimed. "A team of ghost hunters came in to investigate.

They did their thing and said that they picked up on a guy dressed in black, with coattails, who sits there watching movies. He doesn't like it when people are in the theater and leaves when it's crowded."

Horne was surprised that the story he heard from his former manager oddly matched the description of the middle-aged man wearing black from the paranormal investigation team. In addition to the sightings of the gentleman's full-bodied apparition, alleged poltergeist activity has been reported involving keys and lights mysteriously turning on and off. One employee claimed that his key chain was unclipped from his belt, levitated before his eyes, and then disappeared. They found the keys hours later in a room that was securely locked.

"When the investigators were here, they said one spot in theater No. 3 appears to be some sort of portal," he said. "The former assistant manager brought her niece here. She stumbled in the theater and got scared at the exact spot where the old man has been seen."

In addition to its ghost lore, the land occupied by the cinema in Witch City Mall has some seventeenth-century history. It was known as Samuel Beadle's tavern in 1692. Yep, it's the spot where John Westgate was drinking and later claimed he was attacked by a spectral hog sent by witch-trials victim Alice Parker.

When Scott Porter investigated the cinema for Destination America's *Haunted Towns*, he said that he had a behind-the-scenes paranormal experience that didn't appear on the show. "I felt something tap me on the shoulder and I stepped aside to let what I thought was a crew member walk by," Porter recalled, "but no one was there."

Cinema Salem isn't New England's oldest theater. However, it's arguably the North Shore's most active. It's believed that the movie-loving specter in black relocated from the Paramount down the street and has made a postmortem return to reclaim the corner seat in theater No. 3. Yes, all the world's a stage . . . and all of the lingering spirits are merely players.

Bridget Bishop

If Salem's ghost world had a star, it would be Bridget Bishop. She's regularly featured in books and TV programs. Tour guides canonize her. Bishop's story is reenacted throughout the season at Old Town Hall in an interactive play called *Cry Innocent.*

For the record, she was the first of twenty to be executed in Salem in 1692, and she was the only victim to be hanged alone at Proctor's Ledge.

Historically, Bishop is credited with running a scandalous tavern near the present-day Turner's Seafood. Not true. It's more likely that she's been confused over time with Sarah and Edward Bishop, who ran a watering hole out of their home.

She didn't own a tavern. However, her neighbors believed she was both a witch and a thief.

Compared to the other innocents, Bishop had little time between her trial and hanging. In fact, she was accused and executed within a few weeks. Some historians believe Bishop was easy prey because she was a woman who owned land and defied the Puritanical status quo.

Bishop also dressed provocatively for the era. The fancy lace she brought to Samuel and Sarah Shattuck for dyeing was viewed as scandalous. She paid two pence, but the money went missing and

Shattuck blamed it on witchery. After Bishop paid a few social calls to the Shattuck household, their son started crying incessantly and eventually became "stupefied and devoid of reason."

Cotton Mather, author of *The Wonders of the Invisible World*, recounted that several people testified against Bishop during her trial in April 1692. According to Mather's account, her "specter" would pinch, choke, and bite the alleged victims. One person testified that Bishop's spirit threatened to drown her if she didn't sign the devil's book.

In addition to her apple orchard, Bishop owned a house on the easterly side of Washington Street that she sometimes leased out to tenants. When two carpenters, John and William Bly, worked on the basement walls of her Salem Town homestead, they found "poppets," rag dolls similar to modern-day puppets, with pins stuck in them.

The Bly family, living on nearby Summer Street, also testified during Bishop's trial that their neighbor bewitched a pig they had purchased from her. After an argument involving payment, the animal started having fits. The Blys testified that the pig seemed to lose its senses, becoming deaf and blind. The animal refused to suckle its young and repeatedly beat its head against the fence. The supposed proof that Bishop cursed the pig? It spent hours racing back and forth between the Bishop and Bly homesteads. Yes, the animal went hog wild.

At her trial on March 24, 1692, several witnesses testified that a poltergeist attack took place as Bishop was being taken under guard past the town meetinghouse, a stone's throw from her Salem home and the present-day location of Lyceum Hall. "A demon invisibly entered the meeting house, tore down part of it, so tho' there was no person to be seen, yet the people, at the noise, running in, found a board which was strongly fastened with several nails, transported into another quarter of the house," wrote one eyewitness. In other words, spirits were supposedly active during the nine months of mass hysteria and were so powerful that a wooden board levitated across the room.

With that said, could actual paranormal activity be responsible for the paranoia that resulted in the onslaught of accusations in 1692? Yes, it's possible.

BRIDGET BISHOP'S HAUNT: LYCEUM HALL

Turner's Seafood, located in Salem's historic Lyceum Hall, is believed to be the site of Bridget Bishop's apple orchard. It's also the spot where locals believe the innocent woman's residual energy still lingers.

Years later, the historic lecture hall was built on Bishop's land. Nathaniel Hawthorne was appointed the corresponding secretary of the Salem Lyceum in 1848. Guests who came to speak that season included Ralph Waldo Emerson, Henry David Thoreau, and Louis Agassiz. Apparently, Hawthorne had a tinge of stage fright and refused to actually go to the podium to speak. In addition to Hawthorne's literary friends, Alexander Graham Bell gave a spirited lecture at the 43 Church Street location. In fact, the historic building is where Bell first revealed his plans for the telephone.

The site hosted vaudeville-type performances in the late 1800s, and in 1894 the original wooden structure was destroyed in a fire. It was rebuilt as a two-story brick building and reopened as the Colonial Café in 1935.

Stories of ghostly apparitions have emerged from the old Lyceum building since it opened as a restaurant in 1973. It's had different names over the years, including Lyceum Bar & Grill, which opened in 1989, and 43 Church. Numerous people have reported seeing a woman in a long white gown floating above the Lyceum building's main staircase. Her image has been seen in the windows and mirrors throughout the building.

Terri Colbert, a former employee at 43 Church, shared in a History Channel 2 documentary that she came face to face with the full-bodied apparition of a woman while walking up the stairs. "It was a busy night," she recalled. "When I came up the stairs and looked up, I saw another woman standing on the other staircase leading up to the loft. I was petrified. My initial thought was that it was a person breaking into the restaurant. When I realized she wasn't a regular person, I ran back downstairs and almost fainted."

Colbert said the ghostly woman "was dressed in white and wearing seventeenth-century garb. When I realized it was an apparition, I was scared."

In a 2011 episode of the Travel Channel's *Ghost Adventures*, the crew members picked up what they thought was proof that they were interacting with the ghost of a woman put to death on charges of witchcraft. Also, the team from Syfy's *Ghost Hunters* examined the mirror that may be the cause of some of the sightings. However, when the Atlantic Paranormal Society (TAPS) team attempted to contact the spirits, an old-school cash register came to life. One of the credit card machines printed out a receipt with a timestamp and the words "good morning." Oddly, the credit card machines weren't set up to print out "good morning."

Tim Maguire from the Salem Night Tour believes Bishop's spirit lingers in the historic building. "It's very common to hear things like voices or footsteps when nobody is around," Maguire said on the History Channel 2's documentary. "Many people watch a woman walk by who suddenly disappears. We've had dozens of photos of faces in the window looking out and hands up against the glass. People feel sadness. Bishop, when she was brought to trial, wasn't treated very well. Spirits left behind would hang around and convey sadness if they were wrongly accused."

In other words, the tragic last days of Bishop's life may have psychically left an imprint on the environment.

Colbert, who witnessed poltergeist activity in the building like chairs being moved, said she believes Bishop's ghost is determined to set the record straight. "She wouldn't like the idea that people thought she was a witch," she said. "I still think Bridget Bishop is still around here professing her innocence."

Many people have reported fainting or feeling uneasy in the area behind the Lyceum. Paranormal investigators have picked up a high level of electromagnetic activity in the courtyard space behind the building. It's possible that this inexplicably high level of energy is related to the recurring reports of paranormal activity. Some claim they've smelled apple blossoms, and others have seen the forbidden fruit strategically placed around the historic structure. For the record, there are no apple trees near the Lyceum.

One group practicing Wicca in the city conducted a circle at a private Halloween party on the second floor of the Lyceum Bar

& Grill. According to lore, they were trying to communicate with the spirit of Hecate, the Greek goddess of magic and necromancy, as well as Bishop. Instead, they summoned the spirit of a young girl whom they call Annabelle. In fact, there's an infamous picture of the ghost girl, who reportedly has long, wavy hair and looks similar to the antagonist from the movie *The Ring*, at Crow Haven Corner on Essex Street. Some say the teen spirit still inhabits the buildings in Salem and has been seen in reflections on the various storefronts in the downtown area.

George Jacobs Sr.

Based on representations of witch-trials victim George Jacobs Sr., specifically in Arthur Miller's *The Crucible*, the elderly man in his seventies was thrown under the oxcart by the Salem Village community as well as his family. Not only was Jacobs accused of being a wizard, but his son George Jacobs Jr. and daughter-in-law Rebecca were brought in for questioning along with his granddaughter Margaret.

In the pretrial hearings of Jacobs Sr. at Thomas Beadle's tavern, Margaret confessed under pressure from authorities to finger her grandfather and the Reverend George Burroughs, a former minister of Salem Village who was also hanged. Although she later recanted the coerced confession, Jacobs was executed on August 19, 1692.

Meanwhile, twelve-year-old Margaret barely escaped execution because she was too ill to stand trial. With his case, the hysteria literally pitted family members against each other. However, it was the granddaughter—not the strong-willed Jacobs—who seemed devastated by the pretrial hearings.

The famous painting by Thompkins H. Matteson from 1855 titled *Trial of George Jacobs, August 5, 1692,* captured the emotion of the interrogation. However, it's somewhat inaccurate. Jacobs is portrayed as a vulnerable elderly man who was apparently brought to his knees when he was accused of witchcraft. While his execution was particularly heartbreaking, he was not a defenseless grandfather. Yes, Jacobs reportedly needed two canes to walk, but his words cut like daggers. Apparently, he was a feisty one.

Jacobs was known for having a violent temper. In fact, he was charged and fined in 1677 for striking a fellow villager, John Tomkins. According to testimony by John Waters and Stephen Small, Jacobs was held back during the attack but was able to land "one blow and if the latter had not held him by the arms, he would have struck him some more, he being in such a passion," reported *The New England Magazine*.

Kelly Daniell, archivist with the Peabody Historical Society, told me that it's probably inaccurate to portray Jacobs as a helpless old man. "Looking back at the Salem witch trials with twenty-first-century eyes, there was this male patriarchal thing going on. So it wouldn't be unusual for Giles Corey, John Proctor, and George Jacobs to be these gruff, hypermasculine men. They were not soft around the edges," Daniell told me.

"They were carving out a life during the Colonial era in a savage land. It was a very hard existence. It's not an easy life they were living," Daniell explained. "It's also hard for people to understand why they believed in demons, devils, and witches. They were living on the edge of a very frightening frontier. There were animals waiting for them in the woods and the threat of Native American attacks."

In *The Crucible*, Jacobs was portrayed as a spectral predator and was accused of sending his spirit through a window to lie on the afflicted Putnam girl. According to historian Margo Burns, it was quite the opposite. "Women such as Bridget Bishop were accused of sending their spirits into men's bedrooms to lie on them," Burns wrote in the online essay "Arthur Miller's *The Crucible*: Fact & Fiction." "In that period, women were perceived as the lusty, sexual creatures whose allure men must guard against."

According to Charles W. Upham in *Salem Witchcraft*, Jacobs was a defiant and somewhat imposing man. "He is represented in the evidence as 'very gray-headed'; and he must have been quite infirm, for he walked with two staffs," wrote Upham in 1867. "His hair was in long, thin, white locks; and, as he was uncommonly tall of stature, he must have had a venerable aspect. The examination shows that his faculties were vigorous, his bearing fearless, and his utterances strong and decided."

When he was accused by his servant, Sarah Churchill, Jacobs vehemently proclaimed his innocence. "You tax me for a wizard, you may as well tax me for a buzzard," Jacobs responded. "I have done no harm."

His gravestone, memorializing what is believed to be his remains at the Rebecca Nurse Homestead cemetery in Danvers, captures the essence of Jacobs's defiant character. "Well burn me, or hang me," Jacobs emoted at his examination. "I will stand in the truth of Christ."

His famous words are etched into his memorial marker.

GEORGE JACOBS'S HAUNT: REBECCA NURSE HOMESTEAD CEMETERY

If it's true that there is a postmortem unrest associated with the proper burial of skeletal remains, then witch-trials victim George Jacobs may be hanging around the Rebecca Nurse Homestead cemetery in Danvers. The backstory behind what historians believe could be the seventy-two-year-old farmer's remains is a strange one.

"From what I hear, the bones were dug up and kept in a box for a long time at the Danvers Historical Society," explained Kelly Daniell, archivist with the Peabody Historical Society. "They were interred where we think Rebecca Nurse was buried."

According to Charles W. Upham, Jacobs's bones were exhumed in the 1800s and then buried back in the same spot in present-day Danversport next to the river. "The tradition has descended through the family, that the body, after having been obtained at the place of execution, was strapped by a young grandson on the back of a horse, brought home to the farm, and buried beneath the shade of his own trees," explained Upham in *Salem Witchcraft*. "Two sunken and weather-worn stones marked the spot. There the remains rested until 1864, when they were exhumed."

The body, said to have a tall skeletal frame, was accidentally uncovered again in the early 1950s by bulldozers after Jacobs's property had been sold. The remains were kept in a winter crypt at a local cemetery and then handed over to historian Richard Trask in the late 1960s. "Safeguarded for years by Danvers officials, the skeleton was quietly reburied on the Rebecca Nurse farm, complete with replica seventeenth-century coffin and gravestone, in 1992," confirmed Emerson W. Baker in *A Storm of Witchcraft*. "Although analysis of the remains established that they were those of an old man and generally fit Jacob's description, it will never know whether they really were those of Jacobs."

For the record, Trask "safeguarded" the bones in a glass case designed for an antique ship and stored them in his bedroom until giving them a proper burial in 1992. Yes, it's an out-of-the-box approach to storing ancient remains.

Locals claimed that the ghost of George Jacobs once haunted the location of his former home and gravesite on Margin Street in Danvers. "Following the 1950s disinterment, there were no further sightings of Jacobs's spirit near the river, but many believe the convicted wizard's spirit follows his bones," wrote Lee Holloway in the online article "Ghosts of the Salem Witch Trials." "The isolated family graveyard in which George Jacobs now lies is situated in a copse of trees on the Rebecca Nurse homestead and for several years, there have been reports of an apparent phantom in the burial ground."

Holloway reported that there have been multiple sightings of a male spirit lurking in the wooded area behind the cemetery. "One such sighting occurred August 19, 1999, when a group of visitors walking from the house toward the cemetery saw what one later described as 'a man in dark clothes.' They initially assumed it was one of the Danvers Alarm List militiamen who operate the Nurse farm, but as they neared the burial ground, the figure vanished," she wrote, adding that one of the women who spotted the spirit checked with a worker in the gift shop. "I'm the only one on the estate today," the volunteer maintained. "Maybe it was the ghost of old George Jacobs."

Strangely, the face-to-face encounter was on the anniversary of Jacobs's execution. He was hanged at Proctor's Ledge on August 19, 1692.

Based on a recent visit to the cemetery behind the Nurse property, I strongly believe that the land is haunted, specifically near the memorial which also includes the remains of several Putnam family members. Walking into the Nurse family burial ground, you could feel an energy shift. I also sensed a male presence there and actually saw an outline of a man when I shot photos of Jacobs's gravestone.

It felt like someone was peering at me from the woods behind the burial ground. Was it Jacobs? Perhaps. Based on ghost lore, hauntings have been associated with the lack of proper burial or a later desecration of the grave. Yes, it's possible that the witch-trials victim is watching over his remains and lurking in the shadows of the wooded area behind them.

Mary Easty

Why does pop culture continue to pick on witch-trials victim Mary Easty? One of the three Towne sisters accused of witchcraft, Easty was related to two innocent women: Rebecca Nurse, who was hanged on July 19, 1692, and Sarah Cloyce, who was arrested and put in jail but wasn't executed. Their mother, Joanna Blessing Towne, was also blamed for dabbling in the craft around 1670, twenty-two years before the Salem witch trials.

However, according to several works of fiction, there seems to be something about Mary.

For some mysterious reason, Easty is often cited in movies like *The Conjuring* as someone who secretly practiced witchcraft and then passed down the Towne family's tricks of the trade. In fact, the movie's fictionalized version of paranormal investigator Lorraine Warren claimed that the demon spirit Bathsheba Sherman was a descendant of Easty.

It's not true. But why do they keep blaming Mary?

Born in Yarmouth, England, Easty and her family moved to the Massachusetts Bay Colony between 1638 and 1640, and she eventually married wealthy Topsfield farmer and barrel maker Isaac Easty in 1655. The couple had seven children and owned one of the largest farms in Salem Village.

Easty's mother, Joanna Towne, was embroiled in a battle two decades before the Salem witch trials in a public debate involving a new minister, the Reverend Thomas Gilbert, from Scotland. The Gould family claimed that the seventy-five-year-old widow was a witch after she publicly supported Reverend Gilbert. The claims against Towne in 1670 were quickly shot down. However, it didn't diminish her reputation for being outspoken and challenging the status quo.

In 1692 the Putnam family was among the primary accusers. It should be no surprise that the Putnam clan from Salem Village were close friends with the Goulds. And, to exacerbate the tensions even more with the future accusers of the Towne sisters, Easty's husband testified against the Putnams in 1686 in a charge involving tree harvesting within the Topsfield boundary.

Easty was accused of witchcraft because she was a Towne. It was guilt by association. She wasn't a secret witch who sacrificed children in the woods. In contrast, she was a kind-hearted woman in her late fifties who was so charismatic that she even charmed her jailers in Ipswich and Boston.

Contrary to her portrayal on the silver screen, Easty didn't earn a degree in hex education.

Arrested for witchcraft in April 1692, Easty was initially released on her own recognizance after the pretrial hearings but was brought back two days later after one of her accusers, Mercy Lewis, started having fits. Most of the accusations against her involved "spectral evidence," or made-up claims that Easty's spirit tormented them.

Margo Burns, associate editor and project manager of *Records of the Salem Witch-Hunt,* gave a great description of the over-the-top phenomenon. "The basic premise of spectral evidence is that a person, a witch, could send their spirit, their image, from their physical body to somebody at a distance to do their afflicting," Burns told me. "Rebecca Nurse could be standing in the room and the girls could claim that her specter was coming at them from across the room and trying to strangle them or trying to knock them down. Nobody in the room would be seeing this but the girls."

In other words, it's all creative fiction, much like the weird claim that Easty had ties to the demon-haunted witch Bathsheba in *The Conjuring*. Of course, Hollywood isn't the only offender.

Horror writer H. P. Lovecraft, who liked to incorporate New England history and folklore into his stories, received a bizarre fan letter "from a curious old lady in Boston, a direct lineal descendant of the Salem witch Mary Easty, who was hanged on Gallows Hill Aug. 19, 1692. She hints at strange gifts and traditions handed down in her family," Lovecraft wrote to his friend Clark Ashton Smith on March 22, 1929. "She sent several modernly gruesome legends lately, but in general I find it more natural to invent cosmic horrors of my own than to utilize actual folklore incidents," Lovecraft continued.

Even if the flapper-era witch had familial ties to Easty, it doesn't necessarily mean it gave her magical powers. "One of the most frustrating and outlandish myths I've encountered is the idea that people with genetic lineage related to victims of the witch trials are somehow more magical," tour guide Thomas O'Brien Vallor told me. "The victims of the witch trials were definitely not witches. No educated person in Salem or elsewhere believes that they were, but there are a small amount of annoying people that think they were."

Apparently, Lovecraft believed the hype. The mysterious woman from Boston with supposed ties to Easty died in 1933. We will never know for sure whether they were related.

What we do know is that Easty was hanged on September 22, 1692, along with seven other innocent victims. According to Robert Calef in his book *More Wonders of the Invisible World*, the middle Towne sister was beloved by the Salem Village community until the bitter end.

"Mary Easty, sister also to Rebecca Nurse, when she took her last farewell of her husband, children and friends, was, as is reported by them present, as serious, religious, distinct and affectionate as could well be exprest, drawing tears from the eyes of almost all present," Calef recorded.

According to local legend, it's believed Easty's body was retrieved and later buried in an unmarked grave somewhere near Salem's Proctor's Ledge.

MARY EASTY'S HAUNT: PEIRCE FARM AT WITCH HILL

My first experience at the picturesque Peirce Farm at Witch Hill in Topsfield was at a Victorian-themed ghost story event the night before Halloween in 2016. Sponsored by Essex Heritage, the fundraiser was called "The Haunting at Witch Hill." After chatting with the property's owner, Sean T. Ward, I learned that the estate located near Topsfield's fairgrounds earned its witchy moniker because of its ties to Salem witch-trials victim Mary Easty. In fact, Witch Hill is where Rebecca Nurse's sister hid in fear before being arrested and then carted off to Proctor's Ledge in 1692.

In addition to being the country estate of railroad tycoon Thomas Wentworth Peirce, the property was also the summer home of sea captain Benjamin Crowninshield. For the event, I retold the story of Crowninshield's murder-for-hire relative, Richard, who bludgeoned and then stabbed Captain Joseph White at the Gardner-Pingree mansion on April 6, 1830, in Salem.

My friend Kathryn Rutkowski was responsible for retelling Easty's story in the room located in the general vicinity where historians believe the Towne sister slept (some contend that Easty actually hid there because she wasn't at her home near present-day South Main Street) before being escorted back to prison on May 20, 1692. The site of her arrest, located at 116 Boston Street, is where Easty's son Isaac lived during the last part of the seventeenth century. "The original structure is no longer standing, but parts of the foundation are thought to remain under the current house," confirmed the *Topsfield Times*.

My personal experience at Peirce Farm at Witch Hill was more than spirited. I was stationed in the library, which is said to be one of the most paranormally active rooms in the house. In fact, I spotted a shadow figure dart past me during my ghost story presentation. After my lackluster attempt at spooky storytelling, Ward gave us a private tour of the basement, where historians believe Easty hid. I immediately picked up on a lingering energy downstairs that was inexplicable.

When the crew from *Haunted Towns* was searching for locations with ties to the Salem witch trials, I immediately recommended Peirce Farm. The Tennessee Wraith Chasers' (TWC) investigation at the haunted Topsfield mansion was one of three spots investigated for the Destination America TV show.

And it was a haunted humdinger.

TWC's Chris Smith and Steven "Doogie" McDougal interviewed Ward before conducting a baseline sweep. "I would definitely recommend checking out the basement where Mary was arrested," Ward told the *Haunted Towns* crew. "In the office, a staffer said they saw a shadow figure come out of that closet."

Of course, I can confirm the activity in the library-style office because I experienced it firsthand. During the sweep, the investigators heard the disembodied voice of a child say "daddy" in the stairwell leading up to the attic.

In the basement of Peirce Farm, TWC's tech person, Brannon Smith, became visibly excited when he got a direct response from the flashlight when he asked if Easty was there. They also got the word "hidden" on their Ovilus.

From my perspective, the most convincing portion of the TV investigation was in the library when the team picked up Mary's name. For the record, it came through as "marry" on the Ovilus. They also got "sacrifice" and "Alice," which was a perfect segue to their next investigation involving witch-trials victim Alice Parker. As they pointed out on the show, Easty was executed on the same day as Parker, which was September 22, 1692.

Do I think Peirce Farm at Witch Hill is haunted? Yes. Do I believe Easty's ghost is hiding in the basement? No. However, I do feel that there is a psychic imprint on the location which would result in a residual haunting.

As far as alleged ghosts associated with Easty, there was a reported sighting of her less than two months after she was hanged. On November 14, 1692, seventeen-year-old Mary Herrick said that Easty's spirit appeared to her several times, claiming that she was innocent and had been wrongfully accused. Herrick told the Reverend Joseph Gerrish and the Reverend John Hale in Wenham that Hale's wife also appeared to her and was somehow afflicting Easty in the afterlife. Herrick's case was quickly dismissed, but it does raise the possibility that the kind-hearted woman was seeking postmortem justice.

However, it's Easty's beautifully crafted petition to the court begging that "no more innocent blood be shed" that continues to haunt the living. Yes, Easty's spirit perseveres in her selfless plea to spare the others, including her sister Sarah Cloyce, who were falsely accused of witchcraft in 1692.

WICKED PROFILE: THOMAS O'BRIEN VALLOR

"We have a problem with the way that most modern 'ghost hunters' are disrespectful toward the dead."
—Thomas O'Brien Vallor, *Salem Witch*

When it comes to the twisted representations of the witch-on-broom stereotypes perpetuated by Salem's tourism machine, Thomas O'Brien Vallor has seen it all. "I don't find it to be annoying or offensive like a lot of people do because I have seen the industry from the inside out," the Salem-based Witch (capital *W*) told me.

It's the ghost hunters on TV that really stir his cauldron.

He's the first to point out why the city's contemporary pagan population is wary of the typical "aggressive male approach" on programs like *Ghost Adventures* and formerly *Ghost Hunters*. "To a Witch, the paranormal is normal and the supernatural is natural," Vallor said, paraphrasing a quote passed down by his elders.

Vallor contends that the paranormal personalities featured on television don't respect those who have passed. "We believe that the dead are around us at all times, so the idea of 'ghosts' as the souls of people who are trapped on Earth doesn't align with our beliefs," Vallor explained. "We have a problem with the way that most modern 'ghost hunters' are disrespectful toward the dead."

Thomas O'Brien Vallor is a tour guide with the Salem Witch Walk.
PHOTO COURTESY OF THOMAS O'BRIEN VALLOR

As far as the ways paranormal investigators are being disrespectful, the Salem Witch Walk tour guide said it's a long list. "First of all, they don't have the right intention in their heart," Vallor said. "Some might not respect the true history of the area or understand who actually lived here or what happened here. They'll needlessly focus on traumatic things and sensationalize people's personal lives. When a Witch communicates with the dead, it's with the utmost respect."

Vallor has a point.

For example, paranormal investigators wanted access to the city's Witch House, the last structure standing in Salem with direct ties to the witch-trials hysteria of 1692. Home of judge Jonathan Corwin, a magistrate with the Court of Oyer and Terminer, which sent nineteen to the gallows, the Corwin House dates back to 1675 and is an icon of America's tortured past.

Access to the house was denied for years. Members of the Park and Recreation Commission thought it would be in poor taste to investigate the Corwin dwelling. "We have to have respect for the gravity of the injustice that occurred in 1692," responded board member Chris Burke. "This is sort of a touchy subject," said Elizabeth Peterson, director of the house. "We want people to be aware that we're not a Salem witch attraction."

In 2011 the governing board apparently changed their minds and allowed the crew from the Travel Channel's *Ghost Adventures* to set up an overnight lockdown. When Zak Bagans, Aaron Goodwin, and Nick Groff walked into the Witch House, all hell broke loose.

"In broad daylight with [Witch House director] Elizabeth Peterson and talking to her, things got really weird," Groff told the *Boston Herald.* "Zak was filming and the batteries on his wireless mic kept dying. There was some sort of energy causing his batteries to die. We felt something weird, felt cold and then the batteries died."

The *Ghost Adventures* team fought for years to gain access to the historic property. "We've already captured a voice and we just stepped into the house to start talking about history," Groff continued. "I think we're going to be in for a long night of finding paranormal activity."

The crew supposedly picked up a child humming and an electronic voice phenomenon (EVP) of Bridget Bishop, who named "Mary" as her accuser. She kept repeating the word "apple."

In Christian Day's *The Witches' Book of the Dead,* he claimed to have summoned Bishop's spirit away from her usual post at the Lyceum. "I didn't want anyone living or dead to steal the spotlight from the Witch House," he wrote. "The team mentioned recording some strong activity on the second floor, but their machines really started to get going once we arrived. Real Witches are magnets for the dead." Day added that he performed a necromantic blessing in the house, which included a blood offering.

Groff, who left *Ghost Adventures* 2014 and is now featured on *Paranormal Lockdown,* told me that the Essex Street haunt was a historical gold mine. "The location, the Witch House, is just absolutely awesome. To be able to walk back in time, regardless of the paranormal activity that's actually occurring there, it's just cool to step foot on those wood floors and experience the environment of what it could have been like," he told me. "You're almost stepping back in time. Whatever paranormal stuff that happens there is a plus to me. It's a cool place."

In hindsight, Peterson said she has mixed feelings about the investigation. "Personally, I was very uncomfortable doing it. I love this sort of thing, so it wasn't the subject matter," she told me. "They were lovely kids, but I don't think they were a good match for the house. When they were off camera, they were very different. When their camera started running out of batteries, they did pick up a child humming. My first response was shock. My second, as a mother, is that it saddens me that there may be a child's spirit here that I wasn't sensitive to or was unaware of in the house."

Peterson believes the EVP captured on *Ghost Adventures* was questionable. However, she's not saying the Witch House is free of residual energy. "There were eleven deaths in this house up until 1719," she said. "Enormous amounts of human drama unfolded in these rooms. My son thinks he's seen things, and I think I've heard things."

When *Wicked Salem* questioned Vallor about Christian Day's use of blood on *Ghost Adventures,* he bit back. "I don't think that Christian's blood ritual was disrespectful at all," Vallor said. "He has a lot of respect for Bridget Bishop and did a lot of work with her. If you think it's disrespectful, then you have a misunderstanding of blood magic."

As far as Salem's "coven of commercialism" disrespecting its past, Vallor believes it's an underlying tension that has existed for years. "When it comes to what most people consider to be commercial or touristy in Salem, I see it more related to the culture and image that the city has had for centuries," he said. "We were the Witch City long before we were a tourist town."

Along the way, Salem transmogrified from a city known for its blood-stained history to a Halloween-themed mecca of magic. But how? In 1970 Laurie Cabot opened the city's first "witch shop," selling a few tools of the trade. Her underlying goal was to educate the public about modern witchcraft and dispel some of the misconceptions related to her path. Cabot flourished.

In response, Salem set up a bevy of "museums" to educate visitors, including the Witch Dungeon Museum and the Salem Witch Museum, while offering a few scares along the way. However, it wasn't enough. So entrepreneurs set up the Haunted Witch Village, which later became the Haunted Neighborhood at the Salem Wax Museum.

"People were walking away from Salem disappointed that they did not get the scare," said the Salem Wax Museum's former spokesperson in *North Shore Sunday.* "Historically speaking, they were overly satisfied. But they weren't coming here just for the history. They want a haunt—to get frightened out of their wits. So we're going a different route. And there's nothing historical about it."

Of course, the Haunted Witch Village faced some controversy when it opened in October 1995. "I recently visited Salem because the witch trials were the only thing I remembered from high school history," said a New York visitor, adding that he was confused "that a town would make a tourist trade out of this horrible event. These are disasters, you don't celebrate them."

The controversy quickly subsided and the Haunted Witch Village thrived. The debate, however, continued.

A similar backlash swept Salem in 2005 when TV Land decided to unveil a statue in Lappin Park of Elizabeth Montgomery's character, Samantha Stephens, from the 1960s TV classic *Bewitched.* "It's like TV Land going to Auschwitz and proposing to erect a statue of Colonel Klink," said a former member of the Salem Historic District Commission. "Putting this statue in the park near the church where this all happened, it trivializes the execution of nineteen people."

The statue was erected despite the minor backlash and has become an icon of sorts for the Witch City. Oddly, the statue's hand is pointing in the direction of Proctor's Ledge, the spot where innocent men and women were hanged for witchcraft in 1692.

Vallor said he didn't come to Salem for tourism or witchcraft. However, he stuck around because he loved the city's Halloween-year-round vibe. "I moved here as a teenager and went to Salem High School," he said. "I hung around downtown for years before I worked in the tourism industry or even knew I was a Witch." He started giving tours with various groups in town, which eventually led him to the Salem Witch Walk. "In order to help explain witchcraft to tourists, I began to educate myself," he recalled. "That is when it dawned on me that I was a Witch."

The tour guide in his mid-thirties believes that the hysteria of 1692 somehow laid the foundation for real Witches three hundred years later. What are the lessons learned from the Salem witch trials according to Vallor? "Don't believe everything you hear or judge a book by its cover," he said. "And, most importantly, think for yourself."

Samuel Wardwell

Actor Scott Foley's mind was blown when he appeared on TLC's *Who Do You Think You Are?* Known for his breakout role in *Felicity*, Foley was told by witch-trials expert Mary Beth Norton that he was related to Samuel Wardwell, the often-overlooked victim from the Andover hysteria in 1692.

"You always think a witch was a woman, but anyone could have been accused of being a witch," Foley said, in complete shock, when the author of *In the Devil's Snare* told him he was a direct descendant of Wardwell. Norton confirmed that five of the twenty victims from the Salem witch trials were men and his paternal grandfather, eight generations down, was one of them.

Foley also learned that he was related to Simon Wardwell, a member of then-general George Washington's "Life Guard" unit during the Revolutionary War. However, it was his ties to the trials of 1692 that led him to Salem's Witch House, also known as the Jonathan Corwin House on Essex Street.

The actor was greeted by Margo Burns, a local historian who's also related to a victim of the Salem witch trials, Rebecca Nurse. Burns had Foley read testimony by Martha Sprague, an afflicted girl who accused Wardwell of "sticking pins in her" and "striking her down." According to a copy of the original document, Sprague accused the father of seven children of being a "wizard" on September 14, 1692.

"When we talk about the afflicted girls, they were very dramatic," Burns told Foley on *Who Do You Think You Are?* in 2016. "They would show that they were being stuck with pins and they would screech. It was dramatic theater. But the court found this as credible testimony."

Foley also learned that his ancestor was known as the "Soothsayer of Andover" and had an uncanny ability to predict the gender of unborn children. "He had this reputation for telling fortunes and reading palms," Burns said. "We are talking about what happened in the 'invisible world,' which included angels and demons. The 'invisible world' was real to them."

In the seventeenth century, there was a law passed involving people who were charged with "conjuration, witchcraft, and dealing with evil and wicked spirits." Those who admitted to these so-called wicked acts would lose their civil and property rights. Based on historical interpretation of Wardwell's testimony, it's believed that he was forced to confess.

Burns explained that Wardwell initially pled guilty but later retracted his testimony. The original document indicated that he "beleyed" his confession. In other words, he lied. There was a belief, Burns confirmed, that "if you confessed, you were not tried." In fact, all of the victims who were executed up until Wardwell—excluding Giles Corey, who remained mute during the pretrial hearings—claimed to be innocent of witchcraft.

According to accounts from Wardwell's hanging, the executioner at Proctor's Ledge was smoking tobacco, and when the carpenter from Andover was trying to proclaim his innocence, he started to choke because smoke was being blown in his face.

"Good Lord!" Foley emoted. "Everybody in town would come to watch this?" Burns confirmed the brutal reality of the public executions and added that it would take up to twenty minutes for the victims to die with the noose around their necks.

After Wardwell's hanging, his wife Sarah was brought back to the court, where she was convicted of witchcraft and also sentenced to be hanged. Like her husband, she also confessed, and the family's estate in present-day North Andover was confiscated. When Governor William Phips gave a reprieve, she was released from prison. However, Wardwell and her seven children were gravely affected by the witch trials and they became destitute.

Burns sent Foley to the Salem Witch Trials Memorial on Charter Street. During his visit, next to the Burying Point cemetery, the actor mused that his daughter playfully dressed up as a witch for Halloween. "We thought it was cute," Foley said. "It's not cute now." He added that the story involving his lineage meant a lot to him. "From this day forward, I will take his story with me," he concluded during his *Who Do You Think You Are?* journey. "This is my story. It's a damn good story."

SAMUEL WARDWELL'S HAUNT: GALLOWS HILL SPIRITS, ALLENTOWN, PENNSYLVANIA

When Bob Piano traced his lineage back generations to witch-trials victim Samuel Wardwell, he decided to meld his passion for craft spirits and his grim family history, which includes the only witch-trials victim who pled guilty of dabbling with the craft in 1692.

Piano's distillery and tasting room, called Gallows Hill Spirits, features Salem witch-trials-themed decor and drinks. It also illustrates the far-reaching impact the trials had on family with ties to the horrors that unfolded more than three centuries ago.

"In 1692 my eight-times great-grandfather was accused and arrested for witchcraft. He was later hanged on Gallows Hill on September 22, 1692," Piano explained, adding that Wardwell was part of the so-called eight firebrands of hell, a disturbing moniker coined by the Reverend Nicholas Noyes after observing the public execution of the final eight victims.

During a recent visit to his newly opened watering hole in Allentown, Pennsylvania, Piano said that in addition to history, he also likes spirits. Of course, his interest in "spirits" refers to the kind that are served in a shot glass and not the type that goes bump in the night. Well, that's what he initially told me.

The Lehigh Valley tavern owner serves up Soothsayer Vodka, which was inspired by his ancestor Wardwell, who was said to be able to predict the future. At least, that's what the forty-nine-year-old carpenter claimed at first, but he later recanted to avoid execution. However, it was too late for the so-called Soothsayer of Andover.

Piano became entranced by his family's history after doing a search for his mother on Ancestry.com. The discovery of his familial ties to the witch trials was by accident. "It didn't pass down in my family's history," he said about his connection to Wardwell. "I was initially looking for two family members who were on the *Mayflower*. It turns out they were on the *Mayflower* but they were my uncles. There was no direct lineage. While doing research, I noticed there was a Samuel Wardwell listed and noticed his death date."

And the rest, as they say, was history.

For the record, Piano's ancestor is one of three victims from Andover. The land, known as North Andover today, has the morbid claim to fame as the town with the most people who were questioned about practicing witchcraft in 1692. Wardwell's wife Sarah and his daughter Mercy were among the accused. Approximately fifty-one innocent people were arrested in Andover in 1692.

At Piano's Pennsylvania-based tasting room, visitors can sip handcrafted spirits like Tituba's Silver rum at barrel-style tables while learning about the witch trials. "It's part museum and part old-timey tavern," he told me, showing off a wall paying homage to the twenty witch-trials victims as well as the restored indictment of Piano's great-grandfather generations down.

Behind the bar is a convincing reproduction of the facade of Salem's Witch House, which was the home of magistrate Jonathan Corwin. He presided over most of the trials along with John Hathorne. Customers are greeted by an almost original-size replica of the Witch House sign that currently stands on the corner of Essex Street in Salem, a mere 350 miles away from Gallows Hill Spirits in Allentown.

Piano told me he was initially interested in reproducing Rebecca Nurse's homestead, but felt drawn to the only structure still standing in Salem with direct ties to the trials. In fact, he matched the colors of the Witch House perfectly using a "color capture" app during a recent visit with his daughter. "It was important for me to be as historically accurate as possible," Piano said.

As he was giving me a tour of his museum-like craft distillery, Piano said that a psychic-medium told him that Gallows Hill Spirits is possibly haunted. "During our grand opening, we had a CO_2 line explode while I was sitting here talking to local politicians and state representatives," he said with a laugh. "I had a medium in recently, and she did a gallery reading on a Sunday afternoon. She said that she was picking up a lot of activity on the property, but she said the building isn't old enough to be haunted. She seemed to think it was related to the land."

Could the paranormal activity at Gallows Hill Spirits be related to Piano's ancestor? "It could very well be Samuel Wardwell," he said with a sheepish grin. "Not only did the CO_2 line explode, but we had the lights mysteriously flicker and then turn on and off."

Perhaps the "Soothsayer of Andover" was paying a postmortem visit while downing a few spirits with his grandson ten generations down. Bottoms up.

Sarah Good

Reduced to poverty because of her first husband's debt, the pregnant Sarah Good and her young daughter were penniless and possibly homeless in early 1692. Creditors seized her homestead after she married her second husband, William. According to local legend, she would knock on doors begging for supplies. When Good approached the Reverend Samuel Parris, he turned her away. Was it that encounter at the Parris homestead that ultimately resulted in her demise? Possibly.

Good was accused of witchcraft on March 6, 1692, by Abigail Williams and Elizabeth Parris, the original afflicted girl and daughter of Reverend Parris. The two accusers claimed that they had been bitten, pinched, and abused by Good's specter.

After being sent to Constable George Locker's home in Ipswich to await trial, Good escaped and was transferred to the deplorable Witch Gaol in Salem Town on March 5, 1692.

Meanwhile, Good's five-year-old daughter Dorothy, written incorrectly as "Dorcas" on the warrant for her arrest, was questioned because she supposedly caused repeated bites on the arms of the afflicted girls. The youngest person to be jailed for witchcraft, she was sent to the prison keeper's house in Salem. She was then visited by town officials. It was during the interrogations that Dorothy claimed that she owned a snake given to her by her mother. The officials interpreted the child's claims as witchcraft and believed that her pet was a "familiar," a witch's spiritual sidekick.

Both Good and her daughter were sent to various prisons, including Boston, throughout the trials. It was while in the Boston jail that the elder Good supposedly cursed Mercy Short.

In May 1692 Short was delivering supplies to the prisoners when the homeless mother supposedly hexed her. "When Sarah Good asked her for tobacco, Mercy snatched a handful of shavings from the floor and hurled them at the woman," wrote Marilynne Roach in her day-by-day account called *The Salem Witch Trials*. Short fell into "fits and torments" after the encounter with Good. In fact, she testified that she was unable to eat for twelve days and suffered from seizure-like fits. It was supposedly so bad that Cotton Mather's congregation in the North End repeatedly prayed for the accuser.

On June 2, 1692, it was declared that Good, who was pregnant in 1692 and lost her unborn child in Ipswich, actually murdered the infant. According to the ghost child's testimony as recounted during the witch trials by Joanna Chibbun, her own mother murdered her. Chibbun testified that the child's spirit even called her mother a witch.

Good, who supposedly cursed the Reverend Nicholas Noyes before she died, was hanged at Proctor's Ledge on July 19, 1692. Historians have few details as to what happened to her little girl, Dorothy, after the trials. The child was kept in an Ipswich jail until December, when her dad bailed her out. By that time, the youngest witch-trials victim suffered from serious psychological scars. According to some historical accounts, Dorothy went insane.

SARAH GOOD'S HAUNT:
WITCH DUNGEON MUSEUM

When the late author Robert Ellis Cahill helped build the Witch Dungeon Museum on Lynde Street with "glue, clay and some fifty mannequins," he had no idea its eerie reenactments from the 1692 witch-trials hysteria would also become known for its haunted shenanigans.

Before the popular attraction opened, Cahill's nephew fell from a thirty-foot ladder, and other bizarre accidents hindered its initial launch until Halloween 1979. A rocking chair mysteriously moved on its own, but Cahill later identified the Witch Dungeon entity as a mischievous cat. Visitors also claimed to hear whispers and disembodied sounds. Actresses reenacting the trial of Sarah Good refused to escort visitors into the dungeon because of sightings of a hooded monk ghost.

"He appears now more frequently near the crushing scene," wrote Cahill in *Haunted Happenings*. "I'm not one to so easily dispel their sightings anymore, for, after all, their ghost in the rocking chair proved to be real." The rocking chair incident had a rational explanation—it was a wayward puss in boots—but the numerous sightings of a full-bodied apparition continue to be a mystery.

Apparently, the ghost monk continues to make his rounds in the Witch Dungeon Museum's dungeon area. "If you see a shadow figure moving in the basement while walking through the old Salem Village depiction, don't be surprised when you realize that shadow is not another person in your tour group, but a ghost of a monk who once lived in or possibly practiced his religious profession on the historical church grounds," claimed Rebecca Muller on the website Salem Witch City Ghosts. "People have felt extreme cold breaths of air, and the feather-light touch of ghostly fingers on their arms and back. Others have heard a deep, male ghostly voice humming when there are no other men in the building at the time."

Yes, the building at 16 Lynde Street occupies a space that was formerly a place of worship. The structure's last tenants were Christian Scientists. The museum also boasts the original beam salvaged from Salem's Witch Gaol, a relic pulled from a lower dungeon hidden beneath 10 Federal Street. Some believe the activity associated with the Witch Dungeon Museum is triggered by the enchanted piece of wood.

"I've worked at the Witch Dungeon Museum for eight seasons and have certainly met some characters," said Meaghan Dutton-Blask, a fellow ghost tour guide who got her start in Salem. "One woman was a dungeon veteran and vehemently claims there's a ghost in the dungeon, a male spirit who wears red pants and aggressively tries to seduce her when she is alone in the dungeon. Many 'dungeonettes' have claimed that one portion of the museum—the section showing a repentant accuser later in life—has some sort of presence who tries to push the guide down the stairs."

Dutton-Blask said the haunted section of the dungeon museum is off-limits to tourists, but "the guide may enter the exhibit to try to 'scare' the guests, and often has a hard time coming down from the steps, feeling that a force is pushing her forward," she said. "I personally have never experienced this."

The tour guide said she's creeped out the most by the Witch Gaol beam. "The most compelling story for me is attached to the artifact in the museum," she said. "In the dungeon there is a beam that was a support beam in the original Witch Gaol. The dungeon was one hundred yards from the location of the museum."

Dutton-Blask said several paranormal investigators have visited the museum and have taken photos of the macabre artifact. In the photos, they captured what looked like a woman wearing period garb.

Conditions were extremely harsh in prisons at that time. Prisoners' "rights," as we think of them today, did not exist. Cells were small and without amenities. Prisoners paid for their straw bedding and food.

At least five, including Good's infant daughter, died from the inhumane conditions in the dungeon.

"In 1692, St. Peter's Street was known as Prison Lane and the jail was at the intersection with Federal Street, where a phone company building now stands," wrote Frances Hill in *Hunting for Witches*. "In the 1930s, a house stood on the site, built with timbers from the jail. In that decade, it became Salem's first Witch City attraction, when the Goodall family, who owned it, constructed a replica of the dungeons and charged admission. The Old Witch Jail and Dungeon, as it was known, drew thousands of visitors before it was bulldozed to make way for the telephone company building."

People say that the 10 Federal Street building is home to many spirits who have lost their lives over the years. Some claim it's haunted by the tortured victims of Salem's witch-trials past. According to lore, workers in the building use their cell phones instead of the landline because there have been reports of torturous screams heard when they pick up the phone. There have also been reports of unseen forces touching people on the shoulder and ankles, and several workers reported feeling the sensation of being pushed out of the building.

As far as the Old Witch Gaol, reports from the few who survived the prison without adequate food, heat, or sanitary conditions compared it to hell on Earth. "Nearly everyone confined for more than a few days either attempted a prison break or wrote appealing letters to the court for mercy," wrote Edwin Powers in *Crime and Punishment in Early Massachusetts*. One gentleman, a servant known as Job Tookie, asked to be set free in 1682. "No one alive knows or is able to express what I have suffered since I came into this place," emoted Tookie, begging the court to take into consideration "this sad miserable and deplorable condition I am now in." Tookie's fourteen-week confinement was ten years before the witch-trials hysteria. No one knows if he made it out alive.

Wilmot Redd

Out of all of the twenty victims of the Salem witch trials, Marblehead's Wilmot Redd was the closest in demeanor to the cackling witch stereotype. The fisherman's wife was notoriously irritable, eccentric, and poor. Based on how she was depicted by the locals, she was the quintessential example of a cranky crone.

Redd wasn't a witch. But drop the *w* and add a *b* in its place. Yes, "Mammy Redd" of Marblehead wasn't a sorceress but she sure was cantankerous.

Her one-liners during her pretrial hearing at Ingersoll's Ordinary tavern in Danvers could be viewed as combative and somewhat comedic . . . that's if she wasn't fighting for her life. No one came to support her nor did she seem to get any visitors when she was shackled for four months in Salem's Old Witch Gaol.

Redd's husband didn't like her much either, based on his actions. "Wilmot Redd's husband, Samuel, never retrieved her body after judges sentenced the old Marbleheader to hang until her body went limp on Sept. 22, 1692 before a throng of puritans in Salem Village," reported Wicked Local's William J. Dowd. "Instead, executioners took her still body, clad in soiled tattered clothes, down and dumped it in a hollow grave near Gallows Hill."

Bette Hunt, a historian in Marblehead, told Dowd that Redd lived in a shanty near Redd's Pond and would walk around town looking for work. She would bake loaves of bread for pennies to survive. "She wasn't the prettiest broad on the block," joked Hunt. "She was a cranky old lady who didn't want to be bothered."

Dowd's description of Redd echoed Hunt's less-than-flattering description. "Her smile was said to reveal decayed teeth and faint-worthy whiffs of halitosis," Dowd wrote. "Rags torn up into strips covered her feet rather than shoes."

When Redd appeared before the magistrates, the afflicted girls started with their over-the-top hysterics when they saw her. Initially, Redd's response was bewilderment. When the judges pressed her about the theatrical performance unfolding before her, she quipped: "My opinion is they are in a sad condition."

A questionable witness testified that Redd cursed a Salem woman with constipation in 1687. According to hearsay from Charity Pitman, Redd threatened a lady identified as Mrs. Syms with a terrible tummy ache that lasted for months. Apparently, the folk curse stopped the lady's bodily functions and Syms was unable to "mingere, nor carcare." As Marilynne Roach described in *The Salem Witch Trials: A Day-by-Day Chronicle of a Community Under Siege*, "Wilmot probably used more earthy terms like never piss, nor shit."

Roach said Redd was "grouty," a local term used to describe an ill-tempered person, and she had the reputation of magically making a "bloody cleaver" appear in the cradles of the village's children. "People were sure they saw the cleaver's apparition over a child before it sickened," wrote Roach. "Others had churns of perfectly good milk turn so moldy that it looked like snarls of blue wool."

In other words, Redd was rumored to have the ability to turn butter blue. Local lore also suggested that she would lure children into the pond near her shanty. Her home was next to Old Burial Hill cemetery, which contains hundreds of graves of Marblehead's earliest settlers.

In addition to supposedly cursing children, Redd was accused of flying across the harbor on her broomstick. Depositions from the afflicted girls, including Mercy Lewis and Mary Wolcott, claimed that Redd "flew to Salem to torment them, pinching them while they slept," wrote Pam Peterson in *Marblehead Myths, Legends and Lore*. "Wilmot Redd refused to confess to being a witch, but there was no defense."

There's a memorial gravestone near the water's edge of Redd's Pond, which was named after Marblehead's only witch-trials victim. The cenotaph, situated down the hill from the dead man's dumping ground of up to six hundred Revolutionary War casualties, honors the innocent woman's legacy. According to local lore, visitors to the Old Burial Hill continue to hear the cackles of old Mammy Redd echoing among the gravestones scattered throughout the historic cemetery.

WILMOT REDD'S HAUNT: OLD BURIAL HILL CEMETERY

When I first visited Wilmot Redd's former property next to Marblehead's Old Burial Hill, I was overwhelmed by the picturesque vistas overlooking the harbor and Salem Sound. I remembered seeing a similar view in the 1993 film *Hocus Pocus*, featuring three fictional witches from Salem's past, the Sanderson sisters.

There was a "blood moon," or total lunar eclipse, peeking from the horizon during my impromptu visit that afternoon in July 2018. Based on the "something wicked this way comes" vibe I was picking up from the historic burial ground dating back to 1638, I expected Bette Midler's Winifred character to jump out at me from behind the gravestones.

No such luck. Instead, I got an aggressive goose that kept following me around the property. Yes, the honking noise coming from that bird was like an anxiety-inducing siren warning me to stay away.

I didn't listen to the fowl. I was on a mission to find Wilmot Redd's memorial marker. At first, I couldn't find it. So I pulled out my dowsing rods, or witch sticks, and let the energy in the cemetery guide me.

"Mammy Redd," I asked my trusty rods, "are you here?"

The sticks crossed, indicating that she was. "Can you show me where your memorial is located? I've been looking all over for it," I said, not expecting to get a response. The witch sticks didn't budge at first, but then I watched them slowly move and point over the hill, the site of Marblehead's first meetinghouse. Following the rods, I then spotted the pond named after the witch-trials victim. Her cenotaph was standing in front of a row of old-school gravestones and facing Redd's Pond. Found it.

According to Marblehead legend, there's a phrase thrill seekers said out loud near Redd's Pond in an attempt to raise the spirit of the witch-trials victim. The conjuring chant: "Old Mammy Redd of Marblehead, sweet milk could turn to mold in churn." I tried reciting it near her memorial gravestone.

Redd didn't respond.

However, I did pick up a strong male energy lurking in the copse of trees behind the gravestones. Could it be Edward "John" Dimond, the legendary wizard of Marblehead? A mere twenty-seven years after Redd's execution, the local was known to go into mysterious meditative trances and was regularly enlisted by the townspeople to find lost or stolen belongings.

After Dimond inherited money, he inexplicably purchased the wooded land surrounding Redd's Pond. Some say he was practicing "black magic" near the old burial ground, but the community was reluctant to call the man a witch because they were still feeling guilty from the hysteria of 1692.

Instead, they accepted him as a "wizard" and tapped into his abilities to retrieve lost items like stolen firewood. Dimond also had a knack for predicting impending disasters and an uncanny ability to forecast New England's tumultuous weather. Yes, he was a seventeenth-century meteorologist.

Before a storm hit the Marblehead coast, Dimond would stand on top of the Old Burial Hill cemetery to alert sailors of an impending squall, wrote Robert Ellis Cahill in *New England's Witches and Wizards*. "He would then begin mumbling to the headstones, as if conferring with the bodies that lay beneath them," Cahill wrote. "As the wind increased in intensity, so would the wizard's voice."

It turns out that Dimond would telepathically direct Marblehead's fishing fleet, trying to help them weather the storm.

During my visit to the Old Burial Hill cemetery, I noticed a dark cloud moving into the harbor. It was a sudden change in weather, and I quickly wrapped up my visit with Mammy Redd.

As I was standing on the rocks next to Redd's Pond trying to take a few last-minute photos of her memorial, I started to slip. In fact, I nearly fell into the water but quickly put my hand on a rock to stop the fall.

The culprit? Remember that wayward goose following me around the cemetery? I somehow slipped on bird droppings and almost became a casualty of Redd's Pond. As I regained my composure, I scowled at the fowl as she waddled down the hill.

I'm sure Redd is smiling in the afterlife at the comedy of errors unfolding on her former property. While she didn't present herself to me, she was there. In fact, you can almost hear her cackling from beyond the grave.

WICKED EXPERT: KELLY DANIELL

"I'm among the new wave of researchers piggybacking off of the work done in the late 1800s and then the 1970s. I'm just picking up the pieces."
—Kelly Daniell, Peabody Historical Society

Kelly Daniell, archivist with the Peabody Historical Society, is on a mission to find out where Salem Village's enigmatic son, John Proctor, was buried. Leaving no gravestone unturned, she may have uncovered a few skeletons, both figuratively and literally, in Proctor's seventeenth-century closet.

"When people think of John Proctor, they automatically think of Arthur Miller's play *The Crucible*," Daniell said from her office in the historic Osborn-Salata House in Peabody. "They think of Daniel Day-Lewis with his sexy hair and bad teeth," she said with a laugh.

For those who missed the big-screen version of Arthur Miller's *The Crucible*, Proctor was venerated in the iconic play turned movie as the town martyr wrongly hanged for witchcraft in 1692. In the film adaptation, the yeoman farmer and tavern keeper was portrayed by the three-time Oscar-winner.

"Daniel Day-Lewis was in his thirties when that movie was made," the archivist said. "At the time of the witch trials, John Proctor was sixty and he had eleven children from three wives. At this point, Proctor

Kelly Daniell is an archivist with the Peabody Historical Society and spearheaded the efforts to uncover John Proctor's gravesite. PHOTO BY SAM BALTRUSIS

had a hard life and he had a lot of children. His third wife, Elizabeth, was about twenty years younger than him."

According to Daniell, there is no way Proctor had an affair with witch-trials accuser Abigail Williams, portrayed by Winona Ryder in the movie. In 1692 Proctor was an elderly man and Williams was only eleven or twelve.

"There is no historical evidence that they had any type of relationship," Daniell confirmed. "They would have known of each other, but they didn't live near each other. He was in Peabody, and she lived in what is now the Danvers area. It was a small community so they probably did know about each other, but that's about it."

Daniell believes Arthur Miller used Proctor's servant, Mary Warren, as inspiration for the villainous Abigail Williams role, citing a thin piece of evidence that suggested there was a sexual relationship between Proctor and Warren.

"Mary was working in the Proctor household and was one of the primary accusers in the witch trials," said Daniell, also adding that Warren was the oldest among the afflicted girls. "She lived and worked at the tavern run by John and Elizabeth Proctor. When the accusations started flying, Mary Warren became hysterical. Looking at the historical accounts, it sounded like she was having panic attacks. She's also having these visions and claiming that she was getting touched and pinched."

Warren, whose testimony resulted in eight hangings, was sent to Salem Village to appear in front of the Court of Oyer and Terminer in the Rebecca Nurse trial. "When John Proctor found out that she was testifying in Salem Village, he casually chatted with a man in a tavern on his way to get her," Daniell said. According to the testimony of Samuel Sibley, Proctor referred to Warren as his "jade" and planned to bring her home and beat her. While linguists translate "jade" as a derogatory slur toward women, Daniell said it could have been misinterpreted. "There's some discussion that the term 'jade' implied a possible sexual relationship," Daniell explained. "The second piece of evidence is when Mary Warren later testified that she dreamed of John Proctor laying his head on her lap."

Looking at the case with a modern lens, Daniell said Proctor's relationship with Warren could be viewed as domestic violence. "You have a sixty-year-old man in power with a twenty-year-old woman who works for him," she said. "Was it a relationship or was it abuse?"

As far as the myth that Proctor and *The Crucible*'s villain had a sexual affair, Daniell said Arthur Miller may have thought Abigail Williams's living situation made more sense for his allegory on McCarthyism in the 1950s. "Abigail Williams is a bit of a spicier figure because she's living with the Reverend Samuel Parris," the thirty-year-old archivist explained. "So the idea that John Proctor could be having a relationship with a girl that lives in the reverend's household and she's engaging in some type of witchcraft, that's definitely spicier."

But what did Williams and Warren have in common other than they were both afflicted girls? "Abigail Williams and Mary Warren occupied the same amount of power in society at the time," Daniell said, "which was very little."

Unlike Williams, Warren was an accuser who later became one of the accused. "Mary Warren ends up in jail," Daniell continued. "However, she is responsible for a lot of the allegations against John and Elizabeth Proctor. There is something going on with her mentally and her relationship with the Proctors. She definitely doesn't seem to have liked Elizabeth Proctor."

However, Warren's boss wasn't a saint either. "People always try to compare his real-life character to the one they see in the play or movie," she said. "John Proctor in *The Crucible* is a man all about honor and taking care of the women in his life. Based on historical records, he's not a gentle man. It's suggested that he is a very tall, looming, and intimidating person. I'm assuming he would be an intimidating figure to Mary Warren and other people in his life."

Another misconception that Daniell dispelled during her stint with the Peabody Historical Society is that Proctor was a wealthy landowner. Oddly, Proctor was a renter.

"We were surprised to find out he was renting that property," Daniell told me. "Proctor rented his house from a man named Emanuel Downing. He was also farming the land known as Downing Farm and ran a tavern. He got a tavern license in 1666 to give food and drink to travelers on Ipswich Road. As a tavern owner, he was doing very well by the time of the witch trials."

In fact, Proctor had been successfully running his tavern for more than twenty-five years before he and his wife were accused of witchcraft. One theory is that Proctor was so successful that it fueled a rivalry with the nearby Ingersoll's Ordinary tavern. However, Daniell said it's unlikely. "Ingersoll's tavern was here," she said, pointing to present-day Danvers on a historic map. "Proctor was serving people who traveled on Ipswich Road, which is here in Peabody. They are too far from each other, in my opinion, to be considered competition."

It was Daniell's passion for maps that led her to her ultimate historic find. In 2017 she was asked to participate in a documentary on the Salem witch trials. Maine-based Lone Wolf Media, which produces documentaries shown on major cable outlets such as the History Channel, the Smithsonian Channel, and National Geographic, was interested in Daniell's take on Proctor, specifically what happened to him after he was executed.

During the filming, Daniell may have solved one of the many lingering mysteries involving Proctor. Local lore suggested that his skeletal remains were brought back by relatives, salvaged in the wee hours of the night and given a proper burial after his brutal hanging on August 19, 1692. Based on at least one published report, Daniell intuitively knew his remains were somewhere in present-day Peabody.

But where?

Daniell had access to some key historical documents buried within the city's special collections. "In the documentary we go on this journey to all of the sites relating to Proctor," she explained. "Based on documents in our archives, we found out that he was renting the property where he lived. It's kind of wrong for us to call the house on Lowell Street the Proctor House. It's unlikely that he was buried there because you can't bury a relative on rental property."

However, the historian did find out that the Proctors owned a fifteen-acre plot of land up Lowell Street. "If his family did take his body down from the scaffolding, it's most likely he would be buried on his property," she said. "In the documentary we follow the idea that one of Proctor's adult sons, probably Thorndike, could have taken his body from Gallows Hill and down Proctor's Brook, which runs right by his rental property and directly leads to the fifteen acres. There is also oral history that suggests that Proctor was buried on the fifteen acres he owned."

Daniell's Nancy Drew moment happened while searching online. Her tool of choice? Google Maps.

"This land is oddly untouched," she said, showing me an aerial shot taken from a contemporary online view and juxtaposing it with a historic, hand-drawn map. "Peabody's Veterans Memorial High School is on the property. Based on oral history, he's buried on a corner of land where two walls meet. Oddly, that strip of land where we think he was buried was purchased by the city."

Did they find Proctor's remains? "We didn't do any digging because the land was too rocky," she said, joking that the wooded area is historically known for its after-school parties attracting underage drinkers. "The fact that the land was still there, untouched except for some poison ivy and a few beer cans, is astonishing."

When it comes to the importance of her historical find, Daniell is humble. "We just happened to be the historical society that had the most clues as to where John Proctor might be buried," she told me. "I'm among the new wave of researchers piggybacking off of the work done in the late 1800s and then the 1970s. I'm just picking up the pieces."

II. The Murderers

"It was a cool, calculating, moneymaking murder."

—Daniel Webster

The Gardner-Pingree House, 128 Essex Street, allegedly contains an anniversary haunting of the murder of Captain Joseph White, an eighty-two-year-old shipbuilder and slave trader.

SALEM'S CRIME SCENES

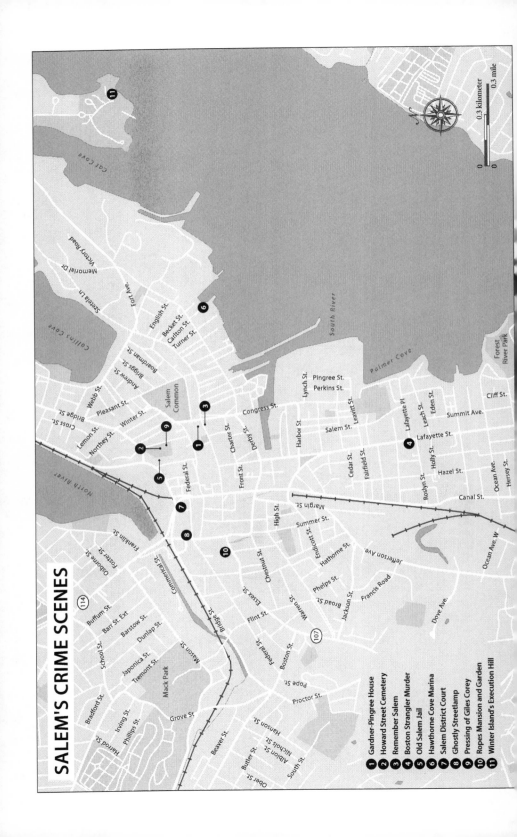

1. Gardner-Pingree House
2. Howard Street Cemetery
3. Remember Salem
4. Boston Strangler Murder
5. Old Salem Jail
6. Hawthorne Cove Marina
7. Salem District Court
8. Ghostly Streetlamp
9. Pressing of Giles Corey
10. Ropes Mansion and Garden
11. Winter Island's Execution Hill

Albert DeSalvo

On September 8, 1963, Evelyn Corbin, a fifty-eight-year-old divorcée, was found on her bed on Lafayette Street in Salem. She was half-naked, with two silk stockings knotted around her neck. Albert DeSalvo, the self-professed Boston Strangler, confessed to the string of 1960s killings that terrified the Boston area. However, new evidence suggests that the Corbin murder may have been a copycat crime.

From June 1962 through January 1964, there was a serial killer on the loose terrorizing women. Thirteen single women were killed and at least eleven of them were victims of the so-called Boston Strangler. While the police didn't see a connection with all thirteen slayings, the public did.

At all of the crime scenes, the victims had been sexually attacked and were strangled by articles of their own clothing. There were no signs of forced entry. It's believed that all thirteen of the women voluntarily let the perpetrator into their homes.

The strangler's last victim, nineteen-year-old Mary Sullivan, was killed on January 4, 1964, on Charles Street in Boston's Beacon Hill. Sullivan's two roommates were working that day. She had the day off.

Sullivan's body was violated with a broom handle and there were marks around her neck indicating that she was strangled by a nylon stocking. A pink-and-white floral scarf was tied in a bow to disguise the wounds. The Boston Strangler also left a card propped up next to the victim that said "Happy New Year."

After Sullivan's murder, it was ten months until a suspect was apprehended. DeSalvo was identified after he tied up a woman and then sexually assaulted her. He then bolted from the scene, saying "I'm sorry" as he left.

While there was no physical evidence to back up his claims, DeSalvo confessed to the murders. He was sentenced to life in prison in 1967. He soon escaped with two fellow inmates from Bridgewater State Hospital, which triggered a nationwide manhunt. He turned himself in and was then transferred to a maximum-security prison in Walpole.

After being incarcerated for seven years, DeSalvo recanted his confession in 1973. He only admitted to the crimes because he wanted the fame associated with being the Boston Strangler, he claimed. The following day, he was found in his cell stabbed to death. He was buried in Puritan Lawn Memorial Park in Peabody.

The killer or killers were never identified.

Police investigators assigned to the Evelyn Corbin murder case have always believed that DeSalvo didn't strike in Salem. Inspector John Moran, a former police detective who recently passed, recounted his initial impressions at the Langdon Apartments on Lafayette Street in 1963.

Moran's first response when he entered the crime scene? "We've got another strangler here," he told *Salem News* reporter Tom Dalton in 2013.

"Corbin had breakfast with an elderly female tenant on the first floor that morning before going back to her apartment around

9:30 a.m., according to Salem police files. That was the last time she was seen alive," reported Dalton. "When police entered the apartment, they found Corbin on a bed, half-naked, with two silk stockings knotted around her neck."

Moran, who retired in 1981 as a lieutenant, told Dalton that he is convinced that DeSalvo didn't murder Corbin. "I think it was a copy-cat, and there was more than one," Moran said. "Of course, DeSalvo went and confessed to all of the cases and how he got in. I never, ever bought him on any of them."

The evidence that haunted Moran for years? It involved donuts. When he investigated how the murderer was able to break into the apartment, he found two donuts on the fire escape, "like somebody was going to climb in the window and didn't want to crush [them]," the detective recalled.

Moran then questioned a twenty-five-year-old man from Lynn. The suspect had stayed at a friend's apartment close to the crime scene and reportedly put a couple of donuts in his pocket, according to a witness, the morning of the murder. The suspect also left Salem the day after the slaying and mysteriously drove to Hudson, New York, with a sixteen-year-old girl in his car.

According to the *Salem News* article, Moran was never able to charge the Lynn man with Corbin's murder. DeSalvo confessed in 1964. In hindsight, the late, great Moran believed the two donuts found at the crime scene was enough to raise a few red flags.

DeSalvo was exhumed from his gravesite in Peabody to test his DNA. According to the forensic report, he did kill Mary Sullivan in Boston.

But what about Evelyn Corbin in Salem?

ALBERT DeSALVO'S HAUNT: OLD SALEM JAIL

Salem's reportedly haunted correctional facility, which is believed to be the site of an estimated fifty hangings, has a long history of housing human monsters. Its lineup of usual suspects included Albert DeSalvo for a short stint, hit man Joseph "The Animal" Barboza, former Mafia underboss Genaro Angiulo, and Brinks robber Joseph J. "Specs" O'Keefe.

Conditions in the Old Salem Jail, which has oddly been refurbished into posh apartments, were notoriously horrific.

"It was a place that didn't have electricity or plumbing, even in the 1960s and 1970s," said Tim Maguire from the Salem Night Tour. "Atrocities happened there, more so than executions, and they would kill each other in the prison because the conditions were so unbearable."

The granite-walled jail and Federal-style keeper's house opened in 1813 next to the Howard Street Cemetery, where Giles Corey was crushed to death in 1692. The building was expanded in 1884, at which time its signature Gothic, Victorian, and mosque cupolas were placed on the roof. The building's addition was constructed with Rockport granite salvaged from St. Peter Street near the exact spot where Corey was pressed to death. Some believed the rocks used to build the jail were soaked with blood from the 1692 witch-trials executions.

Almost one hundred years later, conditions were so awful inside—inmates still had to use chamber pots for bathrooms—that a few prisoners successfully sued the county because of its inhumane living conditions. When it closed in 1991 after a 177-year run as a county jail, the Essex County Correctional Institute, or Old Salem Jail, was considered the oldest active penitentiary in the United States.

"We have left the dungeon behind us," said Essex County sheriff Charles H. Reardon at a ribbon-cutting ceremony for the new facility in Middleton in the 1990s.

But did they really? For more than a decade, the 31,630-square-foot jail ominously stood vacant. The boarded-up structure became a popular spot for vandals, and its historic facade started to look like a scene pulled from a Stephen King novel. It was during the '90s that the infamous correctional facility near the Howard Street Cemetery became the epicenter of Salem's ghost lore.

Based purely on aesthetics, the Old Salem Jail looked haunted.

"Many locals would go inside the jail and try to retrieve artifacts left behind," said former tour guide Sarah-Frankie Carter. "It was common for people to see shadow people inside and even outside on the grounds. It was an extremely active location, and people talked about feeling a heaviness in the air. The conditions were really bad there, so I'm not surprised."

The riots at the Old Salem Jail were legendary. In July 1980 six inmates turned the facility into a sewer after dumping waste buckets on the floors. When the prisoners were evacuated from the pre–Civil War facility in 1991, they "threw food, lit trash cans on fire and threw urine-filled buckets throughout the jail," reported the *Salem Evening News*. One inmate wrote "we won" in toothpaste on a table in the prison's rectory. According to another newspaper report on February 21, 1991, the mess included "pizza boxes, clothing and food thrown about the jail. Also, windows and televisions were smashed and several walls kicked in."

The building became a "magnet for vandals just one year after Essex County leaders vowed to give it to the city," reported the *Salem Evening News* on August 15, 1997. "The 185-year-old building had again been vandalized and some copper piping stolen from it."

It became a hangout for thrill-seeking locals during the late '90s. "Kids have been getting in there and it's become a party place," said Salem police captain Harold Blake in the 1997 newspaper report. "Someone's going to be liable if anything happens there, and I hope it doesn't fall on the city."

As far as spirits, people regularly heard whispers and "metal-like" sounds echoing throughout the structure when it was abandoned. There was also a residual haunting of what appeared to be a prisoner holding a candle, walking from room to room . . . on a floor that no longer existed and had collapsed years prior.

The jail grounds were extremely active, and several locals claimed to have seen shadow figures and full-bodied apparitions of former prisoners darting across the yard and heading toward the chain-link fence, as if they were making their great escape in the afterlife. Civil War soldiers, who were imprisoned in the Old Salem Jail, were seen wearing nineteenth-century clothing and moaning in agony from war-related punishments. In fact, several prisoners who spent time at the Essex County Correctional Institute said they shared a cell with long-gone inmates, or "residents" as they were called in the '80s, from the Civil War era.

One explanation for the onslaught of so-called spectral evidence from the abandoned structure was that the living were reportedly coexisting with the dead. Yes, the jail had squatters. "People have been living in there for nine years," said former public works director Stanley Bornstein in the October 15, 1999, edition of the *Salem Evening News*. "You patch one hole, they open another. Whatever you do, you're not going to keep people out of there. Somebody could easily be killed in there."

After the infamous penitentiary was turned into upscale condos and what was the sheriff's office became a popular St. Peter Street restaurant formerly called the Great Escape, then A&B Salem, and now Bit Bar Salem, the dark shadows from its past seem to have taken a break. Perhaps their torturous sentence behind bars extended after death, and once the cell blocks were removed and the space was transformed, the correctional facility's invisible prisoners were finally set free. Or the Old Salem Jail's squatters—both the living and their spirited roommates—found a new home.

According to former tenant Amy Butler, she and her business partner found the perfect location for A&B Salem—even if it is haunted. "It would have ended up being a missed opportunity with it being the old jail," Butler told me. "It was vacant for thirteen years and the restaurant that was here before only lasted three years. Salem didn't really get a chance to hang out here and get the idea of what really went on here."

As far as the structure's ghost lore, Butler said she's heard several cautionary tales. "When we were purchasing the building, the previous owners told us a few ghost stories," she explained. "He said he would tell us a few but preferred not to tell us the others."

One encounter involved what looked like a figure wearing a dark shirt and pants, sporting an old-school cap and holding a clipboard. The previous owners initially witnessed this ghostly figure from a security camera. They thought he was a delivery man until he disappeared into thin air.

"I have heard it was a janitorial gentleman with a set of keys and a period-dated hat," Butler said. However, it's believed that the figure is a residual haunting of a prison guard from the old jail's past. "When we were opening up this place, we definitely kept looking behind us," she continued. "There are spots in this building with freezing-cold air. I don't know what that means from a paranormal perspective, but it's cold in places where it shouldn't be cold. It's pitch black in the back. We try not to spend too much time there late at night," Butler said when she co-owned the haunted hot spot.

For the record, these cold spots are signs of paranormal activity. In addition to the freezing patches of air, objects mysteriously break, and lights go on and off by themselves. "We have one employee who works in the back bar who constantly has the sensation that someone is breathing on her neck when no one is there," Butler said. "To be honest, the ghost stories kind of creep me out."

Dorothy Talbye

Puritan woman Dorothy Talbye went from being a respectable member of Salem's church to a despondent and increasingly violent murderess. Her husband complained of her bizarre behavior to Salem authorities, who sentenced her in 1637 to be chained to a post for "frequently laying hands on her husband, to the danger of his life."

Governor John Winthrop wrote about Talbye's mental and behavioral maladies, including "falling [into] difference with her husband," a host of "melancholy or spiritual delusions," threats to kill her husband, and, ultimately, the crime of infanticide.

Talbye was hanged in December 1638 for killing her three-year-old daughter, whom she'd named "Difficult." According to her testimony, God had told her to murder her daughter. Winthrop, the governor of Massachusetts Bay Colony, believed Satan had possessed Talbye. Modern-day therapists believe she suffered from a severe case of postpartum depression.

The woman broke her daughter's neck on a cold October night in 1638. At her trial, Talbye refused to speak until Winthrop threatened to pile stones on her chest. During her execution, she fought to the bitter end. With the noose around her neck, she ripped off the cloth around her head and put it under the noose to ease the pain. She also made an attempt to grab the ladder. No luck. Talbye was hanged.

Why was she executed? Historians believe it was Talbye, not her murdered three-year-old daughter, who was the difficult one. "While infanticide is a horrible crime, the courts have always had a fair bit of latitude in sentencing," wrote author Romeo Vitelli on his blog. "When Mercy Brown of Wallingford killed her son in 1691, she also went on trial for her life but was treated much more humanely than Dorothy was. Not only was sentencing delayed because of her 'distracted' state, but she eventually received a prison sentence since she was regarded as mentally unfit."

Brown was cooperative with authorities while Talbye fought tooth and nail, which ultimately sealed her fate.

With the Talbye murder, the negative energy associated with it has ties to unspeakable acts of violence. Puritans believed evil was present and active in Salem. However, does the darkness linger? Many claim the horned man hides in the shadows of Salem's historic haunts, plotting his sinister return.

DOROTHY TALBYE'S HAUNT: GHOST CHILDREN

Ghost kids? Yes, Salem is known for its spectral youngsters. Some paranormal investigators believe that a few of the negative entities in Salem may take the form of children.

The Morning Glory Bed and Breakfast, located at 22 Hardy Street, literally across the street from the House of the Seven Gables, has alleged activity in each of the four rooms named after witch-trials victims: Elizabeth Howe, Rebecca Nurse, Sarah Good, and Bridget Bishop. Psychic mediums who have stayed in the third-floor Sarah Good suite claimed they spotted ghost children jumping up and down on their bed. Supposedly, there are unsubstantiated reports that several kids have died in the house, which was built in the early 1800s.

Oddly, psychic Denise Fix, featured in my *Ghosts of Cambridge* book, talked about a similar experience with kid spirits in her childhood home facing Salem's wharf area. "I was five or six when it first started," she recalled. "I couldn't go to sleep at night, and my mother wanted to know why, and I told her about the kids in my room. She thought it was a nightmare, but I knew it was something else."

Fix said her childhood was like a scene from Stephen King's *It* or *The Shining*. "These kids would appear, and they wanted me to go to a party," she explained. "In my head, I knew if I went to a party with them, I wasn't coming back. And then the ghost kids were like, 'If you don't go to the party, we'll get your sister to go.' So, I jumped on my sister to protect her, and she woke up screaming, saying I attacked her. My family thought I was nuts."

In addition to the playful ghost children, the Morning Glory hosts a teenage girl spirit with long, wavy hair in the Bridget Bishop room. One former guest claimed on the inn's website that the full-bodied apparition of a young woman, between seventeen and twenty years old, manifested in front of her and smiled. "She was dressed in a long gown from the late 1800s, early 1900s," she wrote. "It was white, trimmed in royal or dark blue. She had very light brown or dark blonde hair, pulled back off her face but it cascaded over her shoulders."

Ron Kolek, author of *Ghost Chronicles* and longtime paranormal investigator, also encountered ghost kids in Salem. "I've done hundreds of cases over the years I've been investigating the paranormal," he told the crew from Zoomin.TV. "I've run into all types of ghosts, some angry ghosts and some children."

One case involving two ghost kids continues to haunt Kolek. "There was a house here facing foreclosure by the bank. We were up in one of the rooms," said Kolek, who investigated with his psychic-medium friend, Maureen Wood. "We made contact, Maureen did, with two little children spirits. I ended up playing hide-and-seek with them. They would run behind a mirror and I would follow them with my EMF meter. They wanted us to find their graves."

Kolek continued: "At midnight, we came across this lost graveyard with just about a half-dozen graves in it. In the cemetery, there were two little stones of children. When we got there, the EMF meter went quiet. Everything went quiet. It was as if they wanted us to find their graves."

Kolek's research team uncovered the names associated with the two unmarked headstones. "It turns out that the graves belonged to two children, and they were the same names Maureen picked up on in the house," he said.

How do paranormal investigators entice younger spirits? According to Rachel Hoffman from Paranormal Xpeditions, they bring candy. "We run into child spirits, which are the ones to us that tend to be intelligent and receptive," she told me. "We generally bring candy or toys as trigger objects to evoke a response. Kids love candy and shiny toys," Hoffman said, adding that ghost kids are more receptive to her compared to male investigators because she's a mother.

"We have a mothering nature," the lead investigator told me, "and ghost children respond to that."

Giles Corey

Giles Corey, known as a stubborn but proud man in his seventies, was famously pressed to death for "standing mute" when asked if he was a witch. However, few people know that the cranky victim from 1692 was also an accused murderer.

Corey bludgeoned a man to death.

Seventeen years before the Salem witch trials, Corey's hired man Jacob Goodale was found fatally wounded. Corey's second wife, Mary, along with Jacob's brother sent him to a local healer, but it was too late. Goodale died. In the autopsy that was performed, the doctor said the farmhand had "clodders of blood about his heart."

Goodale was declared murdered based on the evidence. In the trial, John Proctor testified that Corey admitted to striking Goodale. Based on the proximity of their property in present-day Peabody, it's assumed that both Corey and Goodale frequented the tavern owned by Proctor. Elisha Kibbe testified that he had tried to stop Corey from hitting Goodale with an extremely stout stick, but the landowner managed to strike Goodale with "at least a hundred blows."

Apparently, the hired hand was flogged on a regular basis because he underperformed.

Corey was not convicted of the murder, but he was heavily fined. It was rumored by the locals that he bought his way out of the murder charge. However, it did come back to haunt him.

Thomas Putnam, Ann Putnam Jr.'s father, remembered Corey's checkered past and felt that the ghost that had confided with his daughter could have been Goodale's specter demanding postmortem justice.

According to Marilynne Roach's *The Salem Witch Trials: A Day-by-Day Chronicle of a Community Under Siege*, "vengeful witch specters" vowed to press Ann Putnam Jr. to death before officials pressed Corey in a field near present-day Howard Street Cemetery.

Putnam testified that a man's specter told her that Giles Corey had murdered him years before she was born. "The ghost told her that Giles Corey entered into a covenant with Satan to avoid the murder charge," Roach wrote, adding that Putnam also claimed that the ghost insisted that "it must be done to him as he has done to me."

For the record, Goodale was beaten and not pressed to death by Corey.

In 1692 Giles and his third wife, Martha, were some of the first people to attend the pretrial examinations at the meeting-house in Salem Village. He was curious. She got a bad vibe. In fact, Corey's wife hid his riding saddle so he wouldn't make the trek.

Martha Corey was arrested on charges of witchcraft in March. Her husband was called in to testify against his wife. He mentioned that his ox and pet cat mysteriously became ill. Also, she would kneel in front of the fireplace to pray but never said her prayers out loud.

While he was throwing his wife under the cart, the afflicted girls then accused the successful farmer.

"When it comes down to it, Giles Corey was a gruff person," explained Kelly Daniell, archivist with the Peabody Historical Society. "He doesn't seem to defend his wife like John Proctor does. So if you take the two men and compare them, Proctor had a play written about him and appears to have a bit more romance. Proctor gets taken down defending his wife. Giles Corey? Not so much."

Like her husband Giles, Martha also had skeletons in her closet. She had an illegitimate mixed-race son, which seemed to have tarnished her reputation. During church service on March 20, 1692, the afflicted Abigail Williams claimed to see the woman's specter in the shape of a yellow bird sitting on a beam near the ceiling of the meetinghouse. Martha was convicted September 10 and hanged twelve days later. She outlived her husband, who was pressed to death three days earlier on September 19, 1692. Eleven years after Martha's hanging, she was posthumously restored as a member of the church.

While several married couples—like John Proctor and his pregnant wife, Elizabeth—were accused of witchcraft, the Coreys were the only husband-and-wife duo to be executed during the hysteria.

GILES COREY'S HAUNT: HOWARD STREET CEMETERY

Giles Corey supposedly unleashed his curse at the Howard Street Cemetery next to present-day Bit Bar Salem, which has a past life as a burger joint called A&B Salem. "The rumor is if you see him, there is sudden death or heart-related death issues," said former tenant Amy Butler. "I had a witch of Salem come up to the door and tell me if I see him, it's over."

Butler, co-owner of A&B Salem, said she was wary looking out at the Howard Street Cemetery. "They say Giles appears in the windows of the building," she continued. "I had two women come who said they had an 'out of body' experience at the previous restaurant. They were attached to the table, shaking like crazy. I guess they were mediums, and they said they could feel the spirits in the building."

A&B Salem, which recently relocated to Beverly, moved out of the old jail and Bit Bar Salem set up shop in early 2016.

Visitors to Bit Bar Salem's restaurant and arcade can get a ringside seat to Salem's most haunted cemetery. A large percentage of those buried in the Howard Street Cemetery had a fate similar to Giles Corey, the only witch-trials victim who suffered the "peine forte et dure" form of execution. Yep, a large percentage of those buried there were accidentally or purposefully crushed.

"We did some research with the city, and we found that a high number of the people buried in the Howard Street Cemetery, around fifteen percent, were crushed to death," explained Tim Maguire. "It's so interesting because that was the site where Giles Corey was crushed to death during the witch trials."

The Salem Night Tour owner rattled off a series of bizarre "accidents" of those buried at the Howard Street Cemetery. "For example, the floor of the jail collapsed and killed ten prisoners," he said. "A high number of people buried there were crushed to death because of various accidents."

Maguire was a featured player on the History Channel 2's documentary focusing on a handful of Salem's alleged haunts. The evidence he unveiled on the show, specifically a photo taken at the Howard Street Cemetery, was shocking. The picture looked like a crowd of Puritan-era revelers, gathered in a lynch mob sort of way, around what is believed to be the exact spot where Corey was stripped naked, placed under a wooden board, and crushed to death over a two-day period in 1692.

"Someone on my tour took a photo of the cemetery," Maguire said on the History Channel. "By the end of the tour that person came forward to share the photo they took. Definitely not what we were looking at. There seems to be figures of people standing over someone. Most people who feel like they found the spirit of Giles Corey or have seen his apparition, they think it's a reminder of what we have done to him there."

Maguire told me that he rarely gives daytime tours. However, a Christian-based group requested an earlier time slot one day, and they snapped the infamous picture. "In the photo, you see what looks like flames in the background, and you can make out a couple of faces in the photo," he said, convinced he captured something paranormal. "When we were standing there, it was a nice, clear sunny day."

Over the years, Maguire said he's heard of multiple Corey sightings. "People often see an old man go around a tree in there. It seems to be the spirit of Giles Corey," he said, adding that the burial ground's proximity to the Old Salem Jail adds to its negative energy. "What's interesting about the Howard Street Cemetery is that it was built to accommodate inmate atrocities. It was the only coed jail in the country. Women were on one side, men on the other, and children in the middle. There was a four-year-old boy who served a two-month sentence for breaking something."

It's common for visitors to report heart palpitations or a sensation of a heavy weight being placed on their upper body, just like the stubborn landowner who had rocks placed on his chest. It's also the norm for Salemites to mention Corey's curse.

"All of the Essex County sheriffs who overlooked that property eventually died of a heart-related ailment," said Maguire. "Robert Cahill [author of *Haunted Happenings* and sheriff who lived to seventy] was a firm believer in the curse. He had a bizarre blood ailment they couldn't diagnose. It's believed that Corey cursed the city and the sheriff in blood . . . and we have proof."

And if someone sees his apparition? Salem allegedly burns.

"My friend and I were exploring the Howard Street Cemetery," recalled Sarah-Frankie Carter on the History Channel. "There was a very creepy feeling as we got closer and closer to the spot where Giles Corey was actually pressed to death. My friend wiggled through a fence to see if she could get a closer look at the jail, and I heard her scream. She said she saw a man standing at the top of the stairs. We both had a really bad feeling."

Carter echoed the legend that if the "skeleton of Corey's ghost in tattered old clothes" appears, something horrible will happen to the city. "They say if you see Giles Corey, Salem burns. And if he speaks to you, you die," she said, adding that Salem did, in fact, go up in flames after her Corey sighting. "I was listening to my local college radio station, and they said there were fires in Salem. Needless to say, I don't go to that part of Salem anymore, especially at night. I don't think he gives you that many chances."

Locals believe in Corey's curse. In fact, author Nathaniel Hawthorne claimed that the apparition "of the wizard appears as a precursor to some great calamity impending over the community."

According to several accounts, Corey's spirit was spotted near the Howard Street Cemetery days before the Great Fire of 1914 that completely annihilated two-thirds of the city. Coincidently, the inferno began in Gallows Hill, where nineteen innocents were hanged, and the conflagration destroyed Salem.

"Before the Great Fire of 1914, there were almost three hundred accounts of local Salemites who had gone to the sheriff's office and reported this old man in ragged clothes that they tried to help and then who vanished," confirmed Maguire, adding that he doesn't have solid proof of the lore. "They put enough stock into these accounts that the sheriff put deputies around the Howard Street Cemetery. They actually watched that cemetery for six or seven hours and when they left, the Great Fire happened about a half-hour after."

Apparently, Corey's spirit continues to hold the city of Salem accountable.

WICKED PROFILE: KEVIN LYNCH

"If we took the time to better understand how fear operates,
the world would be a much safer place."
—Kevin Lynch, Salem Horror Fest

Kevin Lynch is in the murder business . . . well, cinematically speaking. As the founder and producer of the Salem Horror Fest, he successfully spearheaded a cerebral exploration of the psychological roots of horror at multiple venues scattered throughout the city, including the haunted Cinema Salem. If that's not frightening enough, he unleashed his monster creation during the Witch City's insanely busy "Haunted Happenings" season.

Salem in October? Now, that's scary.

"I've been a lifelong horror fan and have always thought it was a crime for Salem to not already have a horror festival of its own," Lynch told me. "Over the years, I've produced all kinds of Halloween parties that celebrate the fun side of horror, but once the 2016 election unfolded, I was reminded that fear is a powerful force capable of horrifying realities."

Kevin Lynch is the founder and producer of the Salem Horror Fest. PHOTO COURTESY OF KEVIN LYNCH

When I first met Lynch at Gulu-Gulu Cafe in downtown Salem a few years ago, his vision was clear: Horror movies show us what we fear. Based on the Witch City's four-hundred-year-old legacy of murder and mayhem, so does Salem.

In our initial chat, Lynch's goal with the Salem Film Fest was to challenge the status quo regarding gender, race, and sexuality. "A significant portion of our country has an irrational fear of women, people of color, immigrants, and the LGBT community," the Salem Horror Fest director said. "They're willing to act on that fear when fed lies from leaders of supposed charisma and influence."

According to Lynch, the best horror movies serve a dual purpose of serving up scares while shining a light on the anxieties that lurk beneath the surface of society's cultural norms.

"Fear is an engine that drives our daily lives and can alter the course of history," he said. "We all experience it in some form, and how we react to it can have a profound influence on others. So much of our perspective of the outside world is shaped by how we perceive danger and the unknown. Oftentimes, we conflate the two with dire consequences."

Whether it was class-based violence, paranoia bred out of religious frenzy, or fear of the apocalypse, Lynch said the same fear that fueled the horrors of the witch-trials hysteria of 1692 in Salem is still lurking in the shadows.

"What we fear most is deeply personal and reveals who we are when no one is looking," Lynch explained. "It is us at our most vulnerable, dating back to our pre-evolutionary biology. Whether we freeze, fight, or flight determines the course of our survival, both as an individual and together as a society."

Like the Salem Horror Fest's clever, double-entendre hashtag—#KnowFear—implies: Salem knows fear, and so does Lynch. In fact, he had a face-to-face encounter with the ultimate bogeyman, the grim reaper, on his drive home last June from a horror convention in western Massachusetts.

In a matter of seconds, Lynch's car swerved around, skid across three lanes, slammed into a guardrail, and flipped upside down in a wooded area. Saved by his seat belt, Lynch managed to roll a window open and crawl out.

"It's been tough," he said about the near-death car accident. "It was like a super-volcano of trauma that ignited many years of unresolved issues from my past. I've heard people who survived near-death accidents say that it gave them a new lease on life. For me, it was struggling with the feeling of disappointment

—experiencing ninety percent of a death without the climax. Now I'm just left with the baggage."

As someone who survived a terrifying experience, has Lynch been able to process the trauma? "Therapy helps. If anything, I'm more determined to accomplish my goals than ever before. I've already died once—what's left to fear?"

After the car accident, horror took on a new meaning for Lynch. The film genre helps process real-life situations, he explained. "If we took the time to better understand how fear operates, the world would be a much safer place," he said. "Horror fans sometimes get a bad rep for what appears to be an obsession with death and the macabre, but we tend to be some of the nicest people you will ever meet. We routinely confront our fears and dissect the world's darkness."

For Lynch, the murderous monsters in our collective closet can somehow teach us lessons about ourselves. For example, the Bogeyman archetype—whether he's lurking under the bed or hiding behind a tree in the forest—was conjured to make sure we follow rules.

"The Bogeyman serves an important function," he continued. "Its role is to remind people there are consequences for the decisions we make, however malicious or well-intentioned they may be. Like urban legends, folklore, and mythology, lessons and legends are embedded throughout our history and culture, passed on by those who learned the hard way."

As a gay man who has challenged the community's biases regarding gender expression, orientation, and race, Lynch has confronted the so-called Bogeyman most of his life. "Bogeymen are used to manipulate fear in others, like straw men and scapegoats are used to advance an agenda," he explained. "We see this a lot in how marginalized communities are blamed. It's a strategy to divert attention and skirt responsibility. As with religion, you can't prove the Bogeyman is real or not, making it a powerful tool of manipulation by preying on the darkest corners of our imaginations."

Lynch confronted a local Bogeyman after a photo of him surfaced online, dressed as Dr. Frank-N-Furter, the self-proclaimed "sweet transvestite from Transsexual, Transylvania" from *The Rocky Horror Picture Show*. The picture was used to bash Mayor Kim Driscoll's acceptance of Salem's LGBT community. The photo, shot at the opening gala of the Salem Horror Fest, was shared online by a local conservative looking to shame Lynch and Driscoll. It didn't work. Driscoll was reelected in 2018.

As someone who has been an advocate for Salem's LGBT community, how has Lynch seen the horror genre used in both a positive and negative way? For example, LGBT characters have been portrayed as murderous psychopaths in classic films like *Psycho* in 1960 and even *The Silence of the Lambs* in 1991.

"The problem with films like *Psycho* and *Silence of the Lambs* is a lack of balance at the time of their release," Lynch said. "Culturally, it frames LGBT people as only being murderous derelicts."

Lynch said the horror genre continues to push the envelope regarding race and gender. However, he's hoping to see a positive silver-screen representation of the LGBT community. "While there are more positive depictions of women in horror than any other genre, we're still waiting for gay characters to have their moment," he explained. "True representation allows for characters on both sides of the knife, but we need to see more protagonists and final girls who just happen to be gay and trans without it being a campy plot reveal."

Lynch does point out that a few classic horror flicks tackle sexual orientation metaphorically. Yes, the characters are hidden within the multifaceted layers of each film. "To this day, the best LGBT allegories in horror lie in the subtext of films like *Bride of Frankenstein*, *The Haunting*, *Fright Night,* and *Let the Right One In*," he said. "These films deal with characters struggling with identity and being cast to the shadows."

As far as the recurring ghost motif in horror movies like *The Shining* and *The Conjuring,* Lynch said the mythology usually involves unfinished business. "Ghosts are a perfect metaphor for repression," he said. "Negative energy trapped in time, forgotten and unresolved. It's a voice screaming to be heard, when no one is listening. We must acknowledge them or suffer the consequences."

Lynch jokingly compared the filmgoing experience to a paranormal investigation or a mass séance. In fact, the Salem Horror Fest hosted investigator Shari DeBenedetti from *Ghost Hunters* at Cinema Salem in 2017. "Film shares many of the same similarities," he said with a laugh. "Actors and artists captured by light in motion and preserved in a format set to repeat on command? It's like a séance for the price of admission or touch of a remote. Their stories reveal something about the human experience."

Has Lynch encountered a ghost in the Witch City? "It's hard to know for sure in Salem," he said. "Whether they're costumed or real ghosts, I'm just happy to hang with people who find this city as charming and mysterious as I do."

The *Glendower* Murder

Salem doesn't want to be the next Spooky World. At least, that's what local haunter John Denley, known in the haunted-house business as Professor Nightmare, was told when he set up shop in the city a few decades ago.

Over the years, he's had his hand in a lot of the city's scare tactics, including Terror on the Wharf and the current Witch Mansion on Essex Street and Escape Room Salem on Church Street. His consulting business, Boneyard Productions, helps clients around the world create spooky spaces, and he currently has an office in the city. Denley, who helped build Witches Woods, Spooky World, and Madison Scare Garden, said he's seen a backlash in Salem against the traditional haunter business.

"Salem would rather bury its history than embrace it," Denley said. "From my experience, Salem is indicative of the supernatural, but there's a push to focus on its maritime history. People don't come to Salem for its maritime history. They come here to be scared."

One of Denley's tales from the crypt involves a salty sea captain spirit who yells, "Get out of here!" It's this disembodied voice in the dark that spooked the late Robert Ellis Cahill, noted author of *Haunted Happenings* and a prolific folklorist responsible for putting a twist on much of Salem's storied ghost lore.

"When I knew Bob, his thing was about debunking a lot of the supposed hauntings in Salem," recalled Denley. "People all over the city called him to check to see if their houses were haunted. However, there was one incident that really messed with him. It creeped him out so much, he didn't want to talk about it."

The site? A two-story structure built by sea captain Herbert Miller from a salvaged barge at Hawthorne Cove Marina near the House of the Seven Gables. During the summer, the marina is the hub of Salem's seaside activity. During the colder months, the location—formerly known as Miller's Wharf—is a virtual grave-yard of winterized vessels with boats wrapped in protective tarps. There's also an ominous "private property" sign and a black dog that protects the two-story structure, which served as a "fish-food restaurant" back in the day.

Cahill's friend Mike Purcell purchased the dwelling and said the previous owner recycled the hull of a barge and hoisted it up to create a second floor to what was his summer cottage. The building was rumored to have an odd energy to it but Purcell couldn't figure out why, so he called Cahill. After some research, it turned out that the hull of the two-story structure was potentially a crime scene of a savagely butchered sea captain.

Cahill didn't know much about the location in the 1980s before hearing the voice that haunted him for years. It was a disem-bodied growl that came from nowhere: "Get out of here!" Cahill described it as a "raspy, gurgling voice," and it spoke to him twice.

"There was no one else in the room and the voice had that eerie quality of coming from beyond the grave," wrote Cahill in

New England's Ghostly Haunts. "I felt the heat of anxiety flood my face and body, but I didn't move."

THE *GLENDOWER*'S HAUNT:
HAWTHORNE COVE MARINA

Author Robert Ellis Cahill was convinced the recycled barge at present-day Hawthorne Cove Marina was haunted but didn't know the history of the building when he published *Ghostly Haunts* in 1984. He called Herbert Miller's daughter, but she had no clue. It was years later that the barge's possible backstory emerged, and it was more gruesome than Cahill could have imagined.

After years of research at the Salem Public Library, Cahill uncovered some shocking history that possibly linked the haunted barge to a horrific murder in 1911. It's speculated that the salvaged vessel was possibly a barge called the *Glendower*, whose captain, Charles Wyman, was bludgeoned to death with an ax. He was whacked twenty-seven times according to the February 7, 1912, edition of the *Boston Daily Globe*. "Capt. Wyman was found lying face downward in his bunk. He was dead," reported the *Globe*. "His face and head were covered with cuts and bruises. Blood stains were on the walls and ceiling of the cabin, although there was no sign of a struggle."

Members of the crew, including an old Norwegian deckhand named Bill Nelson, were not covered in blood, and the murder became a whodunit of sorts. An investigation by the Boston police found that William De Graff, the *Glendower*'s hunchback cook, was possibly the murderer. One crew member testified that De Graff said that "Captain Wyman is no good," and the captain was axed to death at about 2:00 p.m., right after lunch. Prosecutors didn't have convincing evidence linking De Graff to the crime, and he was found not guilty thanks to the defense of noted attorney John Feeney. After the trial, the cook disappeared and was never heard from again. However, it's still believed the Dutch hunchback was indeed the culprit.

One spine-tingling piece of testimony echoes Cahill's haunted encounter at Miller's Wharf. According to *Glendower* deckhand Nelson, he heard a muffled scream come from the captain's cabin around the time of the murder. Wyman's ominous last words according to Nelson's testimony? "Get out of here," he recalled.

Two years after the trial, a Philadelphia-based seaman claimed the Wyman murder was revenge. "De Graff had specifically gone to Newburyport from Philadelphia to join the *Glendower* crew as cook, for the sole purpose of murdering Captain Wyman," said John Breen during an investigation in 1913. Apparently, Wyman had assaulted De Graff earlier in his career. "Wyman had physically flogged a young seaman out of the ship's rigging in a rage, causing him to fall to the deck, crippling him for life," Breen recalled. "The seaman was De Graff."

Cahill retold the story of the *Glendower* in his book *Haunted Ships of the North Atlantic* in 1997. During a public speaking event at Purcell's restaurant, a Salem-based surveyor, responsible for measuring the property around the wharf, approached Cahill and told him he had heard a similar disembodied voice growl those infamous four words: "Get out of here!" Cahill was convinced. Mystery solved.

However, was the *Glendower*'s crime-scene hull truly used as Herbert Miller's summer cottage? After doing some research on the Wyman murder, I uncovered a series of newspaper clippings from the 1911 murder. There's one shot of jury members from the De Graff trial, wearing turn-of-the-century garb, walking the deck of the ill-fated barge. Oddly, the pilothouse does look very similar to the current structure at Hawthorne Cove Marina.

"The barge, because of its horrid history, never went to sea again," wrote Cahill in *Haunted Ships*. "I think it was the barge that Herbert Miller purchased for pittance, towed to his wharf in Salem, some 12 miles away, and winched up to make a second story for his summer home. It is, I believe, the spirit of Captain Charles Wyman that haunts Miller's Wharf. His final words, shouted at the hunchback when he entered the captain's cabin with a concealed axe, are forever on his lips."

Jessie Costello

Seen the musical-turned-movie *Chicago*? Meet Salem's Roxie Hart. Charged with murdering her husband, William Costello, the uninhibited flapper captured the world's attention with her reported beauty and outgoing personality. After making international headlines, Jessie Costello was acquitted and immediately headed to New York City to perform on Broadway. Her fifteen minutes of fame quickly faded.

Dubbed the "the most astonishing crime-farce within living memory," Costello's bizarre story unfolded in nearby Peabody. After giving birth to four children, her marriage to a controlling Irish Catholic firefighter became unbearable to the free-spirited flapper. Costello started having an illicit affair with a married cop, Edward McMahon. She nicknamed her part-time lover "big boy" but he was later called "the kiss-and-tell cop" by the press.

Her husband was found dead on the bathroom floor in February 1933. The autopsy revealed that it was murder by cyanide.

But who did it? After questioning, Costello was arrested on March 17, 1933, and was tried in the Salem District Court on Federal Street. For some odd reason, the trial became a media sensation. Apparently, she was a charmer. Reporters swooned over the accused murderer, calling her a "buxom prima donna" and a "glamorous siren."

The fellas loved her. In fact, the all-male jury formed a barbershop quartet and serenaded her with "Sweet Adelaide" and "My Wild Irish Rose" during trial breaks. The court's bailiff sent her roses. Crowds formed outside of the courthouse and cheered, hoping to get a glimpse of the alleged murderess. She would receive hundreds of love letters every day.

McMahon, the so-called kiss-and-tell cop, became the bad guy at the trial, and he was publicly chastised for candidly discussing his sexual relationship with the unstoppable flapper.

Costello was acquitted in August 1933. Apparently, the smitten male jury couldn't fathom that Salem's sweetheart poisoned her firefighter husband.

Enjoying the spotlight after the trial, the "glamorous siren" packed her bags and headed to the bright lights of Broadway. "Costello scored $2,400 for the rights to her life story and another $1,100 to appear on stage for four days," reported Stephanie Almazan in the Line Up. "An adult performance hall offered her a very lucrative deal to do burlesque for ten weeks but Costello found it unsophisticated and declined."

However, her instant fame slowly started to fade. When the offers started to dry up, she reportedly begged the dance hall that she initially turned down to hire her, but they declined. She also found religion. A few months after the trial, Costello announced that she teamed up with an evangelist in Los Angeles. The gig didn't last long. She eventually returned to Massachusetts and became a waitress at a Boston tavern.

Costello faded into obscurity but managed one last high-profile appearance. She died on March 15, 1971, and nearly two hundred people attended her funeral, including the mayor and the chief of police.

JESSIE COSTELLO'S HAUNT: FEDERAL STREET

When Salem mayor Kim Driscoll posted a picture of a ghostly face trapped in a streetlamp on social media, the tweet went viral. "Anybody else see a face in this light?" Driscoll posted via Twitter on April 26, 2017, along with an image of what looks like a man's face sporting a furrowed brow and parted lips. The Voldemort-style phantom in the lamppost was spotted outside of the courthouse on Federal and North Streets. "I must've looked at it four times and I thought no one is going to believe me," Driscoll continued. "I have to take a picture of this."

The mayor called the photo "totally eerie." And, yes, it's sinister-looking.

Was the courthouse's scowling sentinel spirit caught on camera? Or is it an example of matrixing, or the human mind's natural tendency to find familiar shapes in complex patterns or colors?

Paranormal experts believe the mayor's creepy photo is a perfect example of pareidolia.

"When I broach this subject at lectures, I get some funny looks from people who think every picture they take has a ghost in it," remarked Ken DeCosta, a veteran paranormal investigator and founder of the RISEUP Paranormal Group in Rhode Island. "Be forewarned."

Seeing ghostly figures or even orbs in photos and videos and sometimes with the naked eye is known as matrixing or pareidolia, apophenia or anthropomorphizing. Basically, it's an example of your brain telling your eyes what to see.

DeCosta believes Driscoll's photo isn't paranormal. "Matrixing or pareidolia is a brain function that we retained from the early days of man and in its elementary form serves as a sort of defense mechanism," DeCosta told me. "The ability of the brain to try and discern faces and forms out of otherwise chaotic shapes allowed our human ancestors to detect possible threats from a distance . . . in the form of predators that might encroach on their shelter, mates, offspring, or food."

DeCosta pointed out the results of the Rorschach test as an example of the pareidolia phenomenon. "Children tend to see animals, whereas adults tend to see faces," he said of the test. "It kind of speaks to our psychological development as we get older."

Joni Mayhan, a fellow author of paranormal-themed books, told me she avoids the "Is it matrixing?" conversation with her readers. "Every time I post a photo of a haunted building, someone sees a face in the window," she told me. "I would correct them, telling them about matrixing, but I got weary of the ensuing argument afterwards."

The phenomenon is easy to spot by paranormal experts. However, will ghost-hunting novices also classify the mayor's photo shot outside of the courthouse on the corner of Federal Street as pareidolia? Jonathan Grey, the lead singer of the local band Salem Wolves, strongly believes it's matrixing. "It's been there forever and has always looked like that," he responded. "Then someone decided it looked like a face and it blew up over night like the yodeling Walmart kid."

Paranormal investigator Debi Watson recommended that I try to debunk the mayor's photo. "If you can take the picture two or more times in the exact same location and get that face, it's matrixing," Watson explained. "I always take numerous shots in the same spot for this reason. It does look like a face to me, but the inside workings or external reflections need to be taken into consideration."

In addition to writing historical-based ghost books, I'm also a paranormal investigator. So, I spent one afternoon on Federal Street trying to re-create the image that was picked up by hundreds of websites and news organizations across the globe.

While checking out the street, I noticed the old courthouse from the photos featuring Jessie Costello, a forgotten figure from Salem's past, arrested on March 17, 1933, for the murder of her husband. Crowds of revelers, mostly men, gathered on Federal Street and cheered her on as she walked to and from the courtroom and into a limousine. The murderess would receive hundreds of love letters from doting men each day.

Could the ghostly man in the lamppost be her murdered husband, William Costello, seeking postmortem justice? Probably not.

After finding the streetlamp from Driscoll's photo and trying different angles with my camera, I was able to capture several photos of the disembodied phantom supposedly trapped in the lamppost. Yes, I debunked Salem's mayor. The difference with my example of photo matrixing is that the creepy ghost-faced man in the pictures looked like he was smirking at me.

It was as if I was being mocked by the ghosts of Salem. In hindsight, I probably was.

Richard Crowninshield

It's arguably Salem's crime of the century. The murder of Captain Joseph White, an eighty-two-year-old shipmaster and slave trader, riveted the nation in 1830 and inspired literary giants like Edgar Allan Poe and Nathaniel Hawthorne.

The crime scene, a three-story brick mansion built in 1804 and located at 128 Essex Street, is believed to boast a residual haunting, a psychic imprint of sorts replaying the savage murder of White, who was whacked over the head with a twenty-two-inch piece of refurbished hickory, also known as an "Indian club," and stabbed thirteen times near his heart. According to several reports, a full-bodied apparition peeks out of the second-floor window. A female spirit rumored to be White's niece, Mary Beckford, who served as his housekeeper in addition to being his next of kin, is also said to haunt the Essex Street house. Beckford's daughter, also a Mary, was formerly part of the household in the 1820s but moved to Wenham with her husband, Joseph Jenkins Knapp Jr.

As far as the murder, it's a complicated puzzle that has been twisted over the years. Captain White's grand-nephew, Joseph Knapp, learned that the retired merchant had just completed his will, leaving $15,000 to Mrs. Beckford. Knapp believed if White died without a will, his mother-in-law would inherit half his fortune of $200,000. So, Knapp and his brother John hired a black sheep from the respected Crowninshield family, Richard, to slay the captain in his sleep for a mere $1,000. Knapp had access to White's Essex Street home, and in April 1830 he stole the will and left the back parlor window unlocked. Beckford and her daughter Mary were staying in Wenham.

Richard Crowninshield slipped into the mansion at night and "entering the house, stealthily threaded the staircase, softly opened the chamber door of the sleeping old man." He killed him with a single blow to the left temple, according to an account in the April 1830 edition of the *Salem Observer*.

Crowninshield hid the murder weapons under the steps at the former Howard Street meetinghouse. The bludgeon, a hickory-stick club, was "fashioned to inflict a deadly blow with the least danger of breaking the skin. The handle was contrived as to yield a firm grasp to the hand."

As far as the crime scene, White was in his bedchamber lying diagonally across the bed on his right side. Blood strangely didn't ooze from the thirteen stab wounds because he died from the bludgeon, and no valuables in the house were missing. Because there was no theft, police detectives were baffled at first. The Knapp brothers falsely claimed they had been robbed by three men en route to Wenham, which added some initial confusion to the murder mystery.

A gang of assassins in Salem? Yes, there were three, but it was the Knapp brothers and murder-for-hire crony Richard Crowninshield, who later hanged himself with a handkerchief tied to the bars of his prison cell before he was convicted. The Knapp brothers were then put on trial after the prison suicide.

Daniel Webster, giving arguably one of his most famous legal orations, served as the Knapps' prosecutor and called the affair "a most extraordinary case" and a "cool, calculating, moneymaking murder." The Knapp brothers, admitting they had planned the crime and fabricated the robbery story, were convicted. Meanwhile, it's believed that Edgar Allan Poe was inspired by Webster's speech and penned "The Tell-Tale Heart," a classic short story involving the guilt and retribution associated with the grisly murder of an older man. Hawthorne was also entranced by the trial and explored similar themes in *The Scarlet Letter* and *The House of the Seven Gables*.

Thousands gathered in downtown Salem to watch their public executions. John Francis Knapp was hanged on September 28, 1830, in front of a blood-soaked haunt from Salem's past: the former Witch Gaol, or witch dungeon, currently located at 10 Federal Street. His brother Joe, considered to be the mastermind behind the crime, met a similar fate three months later in November. The infamous murder weapon, the custom-made "Indian club" that measures more than twenty-two inches, is owned by the Peabody Essex Museum. Unfortunately, the macabre artifact isn't on display today, but visitors can tour the refurbished mansion.

WICKED EXPERT: JACK KENNA

"If there ever was a town that had cause
to be haunted, it would be Salem."
—Jack Kenna, *Haunted Case Files*

Jack Kenna, a paranormal investigator and author featured on TV shows like Destination America's *Paranormal Survivor* and *Haunted Case Files,* believes that a "nonhuman" entity is lurking in the shadows of the Witch City.

"There is something much older and much more intense that resides in the Salem area," Kenna told me. "It likes to pretend it is something other than it is, and while I would not call it demonic, I would say it has a dislike of humans and is something that I would call elemental in its nature. In other words, it is nonhuman."

Author and investigator Jack Kenna has been featured on Destination America's *Paranormal Survivor* and *Haunted Case Files.* PHOTO COURTESY OF JACK KENNA

Kenna believes the Witch City has an "aura of disaster" which has left a psychic imprint on the haunted location. "Like most of New England, there is a lot of history in Salem," he said. "Some of its history is good and some very tragic."

The paranormal investigator said tragedies preceding the witch trials of 1692 stained the land with blood. "In 1615 the

Naumkeag tribe engaged in a war with the Tarrantine people that cost the lives of many on both sides," he explained. "Then in 1617 a plague broke out in the region, which took a heavy toll on the Naumkeag people."

Kenna said the smallpox epidemic in the 1630s devastated Salem's native population, which tainted the soil in the years leading up to the witch trials. "Then in 1830 one of the most infamous murders in early American history took place in Salem, the murder of Captain Joseph White by Richard Crowninshield," he said. "If there ever was a town that had cause to be haunted, it would be Salem."

The author of *S.P.I.R.I.T.S. of New England: Hauntings, Ghosts & Demons* said his empathic abilities are heightened in the Witch City. "Having spent some time in Salem in recent years and being able to participate in investigations at locations in town, I have picked up on something more than just human spirit and the residual energies of past events in these locations," he said.

What exactly is the "elemental" entity that Kenna believes is hiding in Salem's shadows? "They are an ancient nonhuman spirit that is directly connected to the elements of our world . . . earth, wind, fire, and water," Kenna explained, adding that Native Americans worshipped these ancient elementals and they are still revered by Native tribes. "They are not demons or angels. Elementals don't try to physically harm humans, but they typically don't like modern humans because of the way we treat the world."

Tim Maguire's Remember Salem gift shop, located at 127 Essex Street, is allegedly home to one of these elemental entities. The basement of the neighboring *Harry Potter*–themed wand store called Wynott's Wands, which is the starting point of the

Salem Night Tour, is reportedly home to a negative spirit known to throw items and yell at people who dare to venture below.

"There are places in Salem I don't like. Like the basement here, I don't go down there alone," Maguire told me during an interview at Remember Salem. "I've run into more activity in Salem than anywhere else. Most of my life, I've encountered residual, non-intelligent, nonresponsive types of activity. Salem seems to have a lot more intelligent hauntings, and they tend to screw with people here."

Some believe the residual energy is possibly tied to one of the elemental spirits Kenna talked about. "Several years ago, we heard a man's voice come over our soundtrack in the store, and he clearly said, 'I see you. I watch you,'" Maguire said. "We've had employees and customers see a little girl on the back steps. We've recorded several EVPs, and the little girl is often picked up. She has told us through EVPs that she hides from others."

Based on Maguire's description, Kenna said the entity exhibits elemental-type behavior. "They are guardians of the earth and the elements, and they are found in various regions of the world in different forms," Kenna said. "They will try to drive out people who build homes or buildings or even towns and cities by trying to scare them off through visions of strange creatures and apparitions, constant nightmares, poltergeist activity, and threatening-type hauntings."

The good news? "Elementals don't try to possess people or try to get them to harm themselves like demonic entities do," Kenna continued.

Kenna had a firsthand encounter with the negative energy lingering at Maguire's Remember Salem and Wynott's Wands during a paranormal convention called Salem Con in 2015. He was investigating the two Essex Street locations with a group of well-known personalities in the field, including John Zaffis and Brian J. Cano from *Haunted Collector.* "I was with the first group that was investigating the Remember Salem shop on Essex Street, which is directly across the street from the Gardner-Pingree House, formerly the home of Captain Joseph White," Kenna recalled. "John [Zaffis] knew much of the history of the location as well as the murder of Captain White, although he was very careful not to give specifics or details of the murder."

It was during the Salem Con–sponsored investigation at Remember Salem that Kenna had a face-to-face encounter with a negative spirit. "Upon entering Remember Salem, we moved to the back of the shop where there were two large picnic tables set up," he said. "Once everyone was in the room, about twelve of us, John Zaffis asked if anyone felt they were sensitive to spirit energy. Several of the women raised their hands to indicate that they were. I did not."

Zaffis told the group to go to the spot in the shop that they intuitively felt drawn to during the investigation. Kenna noticed a back-door exit to the alley and another door to the right. "I just felt drawn to this area," Kenna said. "I felt as though there was a strong presence back there. It was a sense of someone hiding, trying not to be noticed and trying to avoid all of us."

Kenna said he felt a presence pacing maniacally back and forth between the doors behind him. "I began to get feelings of anxiety and fear," he said. "These feelings became much stronger over the next hour of the ghost-hunt session. An ill feeling came over me the longer I stayed in that area."

The entity wanted Kenna to leave it alone. "At one point, the anxiety became so bad that I began shaking slightly," he said, telling

Zaffis and Cano about his intensifying emotions. Cano responded, "I've been watching you and I thought something might be affecting you. I don't know if you've seen it or not, but there is a shadow figure that keeps pacing back and forth behind you."

Kenna found Cano's comments alarming because he hadn't talked about the energy he sensed pacing back and forth in Remember Salem. "I only mentioned the strong feeling of anxiety," Kenna continued.

Zaffis felt that the entity fit the description of Richard Crowninshield, the man who murdered Captain Joseph White literally across the street at the Gardner-Pingree House on April 6, 1830. "It was believed that he hid in this area while he waited to sneak into the house and murder Captain White," Kenna surmised. "It's also believed that he perhaps went and hid there again for a time after committing the murder."

Kenna told me that Crowninshield may continue to hide in the afterlife. "I don't feel as though the spirit of Richard was trying to possess me at the time," Kenna said. "But I do feel that he didn't like me finding him and wanted me, and the rest of the group, out of there."

After his encounter with what he believes was a residual energy related to the Captain White murder, Kenna became obsessed with the murder that shocked America in the 1830s. "Given the brutal nature of the crime, I believe that Richard Crowninshield was more than a willing participant in the murder for reasons other than just money," he said. "I do agree with the results of the autopsy. The blow to the head came first and must have killed Captain White while he slept. Whether that was his intent or not is hard to say. It may have been done just to knock him unconscious."

Kenna said the severity of the murder suggested a "crime of passion" and it should be noted that it was investigated before modern-day forensic tools. "The thirteen stab wounds tell me that this was a murder of passion. This person hated Captain White," he said, adding that the stabs to the heart are significant. "The force used to inflict the stab wounds and number of them speak to the emotional state of the murderer toward the victim."

Paranormal experts like Kenna think a murder can leave a psychological imprint on a location. "It's just an obvious fact that murders have a strong negative energetic impact on not only the location it takes place in, but on the people that it impacts," Kenna said. "I do believe that it's very possible that a crime, especially a very serious or violent crime, can and often does imprint itself on a location because of the considerable amount of adverse and traumatic energy that is instantly generated by these types of events."

As far as Kenna's perceptions of Salem, he said that the encounter in 2015 didn't scare him away from the Witch City. "My personal impression of Salem is that it's an amazing historical location and a fun place to visit and hang out," he said, adding that he finds it frustrating that city officials are apprehensive about embracing the paranormal community.

"They don't want to see the city turned into a spectacle for ghost hunting and end up drawing what I think they perceive as a third-class tourism business," Kenna contends. "At the same time they tolerate some of the paranormal-related events and television shows because it brings them free advertising and draws more people to the city during the off-season. It's hypocritical and frustrating from the standpoint of serious paranormal researchers."

RICHARD CROWNINSHIELD'S HAUNT: GARDNER-PINGREE HOUSE

Every major city has one: a murder house. In Salem, it's known as the Gardner-Pingree estate located at 129 Essex Street. And, yes, it's supposedly haunted.

"There were two guys from Oregon who came here to debunk things and they captured on video what seems to be a man looking out of the window," recalled Tim Maguire from the Salem Night Tour. "Of all of the places we visit, we get the most photographic evidence from the Gardner-Pingree House. I've been inside the house a few times and I feel more of a presence of a woman. There's definitely a female presence there."

Maguire said that Salem's murder house is one of many haunted crime scenes scattered throughout the Witch City. What makes this North Shore town so paranormally active? He told me that Salem has an energy that is different from other locations in New England and seems to be oddly electric . . . as if there is something charged in the atmosphere. In fact, Maguire has heard from multiple people that their electronic devices mysteriously drain when they visit. The tour owner said there is no scientific explanation for the electrical issues, or what some call "ley lines" buried beneath the city's blood-soaked Puritanical soil. It's just one of Salem's weird mysteries.

During a recent "Graveyard Getaways" tour I organized for a small group of investigators and paranormal enthusiasts in early April 2018, our crew was able to go inside Salem's murder house after visiting nearby Howard Street Cemetery. The consensus, which aligned with Maguire's observation, was that the structure had an intense, inexplicable energy.

"When I walked into that house, it felt like a very inviting home," explained investigator Nicole Hellested. "As the tour continued, I started to feel like I was being watched. When we made our way up to the second floor, I was overwhelmed with heaviness. I felt uneasy when I walked into the bedroom where the murder took place. I stepped in and then immediately out. I had a feeling that I shouldn't be in there and I needed to get out."

When asked if she believed that the Gardner-Pingree mansion is haunted, Hellested said "yes" without hesitation. "The house has a horrifying history, and I think that the spirits there want to keep it safe and protected," she added.

Russ Stiver, a veteran investigator and a sensitive to the paranormal, agreed with Hellested. "I almost had to leave the location because of the overwhelming energy present," he said. "It wasn't negative by any means, but very strong and protective over the house."

Stiver said he experienced a fight-or-flight reaction as the group inched toward the scene of the crime. "I didn't start to get anxious until I went to the second floor and toward the bedroom," he recalled. "I felt dizzy, sick to my stomach, and disoriented."

Brian Gerraughty, a skeptic among the group of investigators and sensitives, said even he felt strange on the second floor of the Gardner-Pingree House. "I didn't feel any negative energy entering the house or on the first floor at all, but there was an innate sense of foreboding going up to the second floor and especially entering the bedroom," he told me. "But I'm not a sensitive in any true respect."

Psychic imprint from the past? Paranormal investigators like Adam Berry from TLC's *Kindred Spirits* believe that residual energy associated with heinous crimes, specifically murders, has potential to leave a supernatural imprint. "Any time there's a traumatic event, it could be left behind," Berry said. "If you walk into a room and two people have been arguing, fiercely, you can feel that weirdness that they've created or energy they emit spewing at each other. I do think there's a form of energy that can be left behind from a traumatic event or any kind of murder or suicide in a room. The theory is that maybe that energy goes into the walls and lingers there."

According to several reports, the historic murder repeats itself spectrally on the anniversary of Captain White's death. There are also many sightings of a male phantom, believed to be White or possibly one of the Knapp brothers or even Richard Crowninshield, gazing out of the second floor of the Gardner-Pingree House as the living frolic up and down Essex Street. If the mansion's male spirit truly has a calendar, his next scheduled appearance is April 6.

As for the city's penchant for historical coincidences, the family home of White's murderer, the Crowninshield-Bentley House, was literally moved next to the crime scene in 1959. Yep, the murderer's house was placed next-door to the murder house. Sometimes fact is stranger than fiction.

III. The Cursed

"You are a liar. I am no more a witch than you are a wizard.
And if you take away my life, God will give you blood to drink."

—Sarah Good

Nathaniel Hawthorne was born at his father's house at 27 Union Street on July 4, 1804. The building currently sits adjacent to the House of the Seven Gables, also known as the Turner-Ingersoll Mansion.

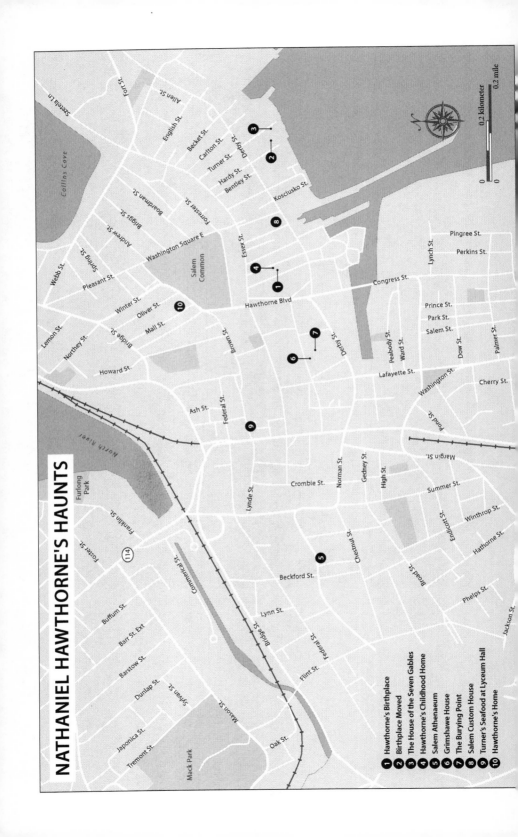

NATHANIEL HAWTHORNE'S HAUNTS

1. Hawthorne's Birthplace
2. Birthplace Moved
3. The House of the Seven Gables
4. Hawthorne's Childhood Home
5. Salem Athenaeum
6. Grimshawe House
7. The Burying Point
8. Salem Custom House
9. Turner's Seafood at Lyceum Hall
10. Hawthorne's Home

0.2 Kilometer
0.2 mile

Abigail Ropes

When it comes to the fire-prone Ropes Mansion, fact is stranger than fiction. The ghost lore associated with the 1720s-era Georgian Colonial home involving Judge Nathaniel Ropes and his distant relative Abigail Ropes has been twisted over time. However, it doesn't mean the Samuel McIntire–designed mansion isn't inhabited by the spirits of its previous owners.

Known for its beautifully curated gardens and brief-but-memorable cameo in the Salem-based flick *Hocus Pocus*, the Ropes Mansion has a haunted history dating back to 1774, when the Tory-leaning Judge Ropes was mobbed by a gang of patriots who hurled mud and stones at the house. The revolutionaries wanted the judge to publicly denounce his loyalties to the British crown. Ropes didn't respond from his bedchamber, and the forty-eight-year-old died the following day from complications associated with smallpox.

Judge Ropes's spirit reportedly still lingers in the white eighteenth-century house. In fact, the mansion's former caretakers, Rick and Georgette Stafford, snapped a photo during an insurance appraisal of what looks like two ghostly hands of a man sitting on the couch in the front hall. Oddly, it's in this spot that Ropes and John Adams argued politics over lunch in 1769. Author Robert Ellis Cahill published the now-infamous picture in his book

Ghostly Haunts. "Here the judge sits for a spell on the front hall couch," Cahill wrote. "After all, if you were wandering around this mansion for two-hundred years, you'd want to sit for a while, wouldn't you?"

In *Ghostly Haunts*, the Staffords alluded to a recurring issue plaguing the twenty-room mansion: fire and the lingering energy of Abigail "Nabby" Ropes. "The burglar or fire alarm would go off now and then, bringing the police or fire trucks," Rick Stafford said. "Occasionally, a dish would be knocked over in the pantry late at night, but otherwise, the Judge and Abigail have been fairly quiet."

The Staffords were featured in an article in the 1980s, and the piece talked about the lore associated with the ghost of Nabby. "At sunset, Georgette works her way upstairs to the draw in the Ropes family flag hanging above the front doorway," wrote journalist George Harrar. "There in the blue room she listens a moment for the screams of Abigail Ropes, consumed by fire when her petticoats caught flame at the fireplace. Abigail's servants never heard the screams for help, or so they said."

Several sources, including *Haunted Salem & Beyond*, incorrectly identify Abigail's ties to the house's original owner. "Judge Ropes's wife Abigail also died in the house. Hers was a bizarre and tragic passing."

Not true. After digging through historical documents, it turns out that Judge Ropes's wife was Priscilla Sparhawk Ropes. However, it's true that Abigail's death was bizarre and tragic. Born on October 20, 1796, she was the daughter of a later Nathaniel Ropes and his first wife, Sarah. "She died unmarried from burns received when carrying coals from one room to another," confirmed *Portraits in Public Build-*

ings in Salem, memorializing her death on April 23. Nabby's obituary published in the April 26, 1839, edition of the *Salem Gazette* offered more details, reporting that she suffered from "a distressing illness of three weeks caused by her clothes accidentally taking fire."

Yes, Abigail Ropes, who received the nickname "Nabby" from her family, became a human torch and burned alive in the mansion's second-floor blue room. Her horrific demise, spanning three weeks, might explain the reports—ranging from a ghostly figure peeking out of the second-floor window to sightings of a full-bodied female apparition with long, dark hair wrapped in a bun—of supposed paranormal activity linked to the home.

In her obituary, she was portrayed as a recluse: "Though mixing little in general society, she was interested in all the passing events in life." In other words, she didn't leave the house much.

ABIGAIL ROPES'S HAUNT: ROPES MANSION

Is the ghost of "Nabby" responsible for the freakish fires plaguing Ropes Mansion?

While workmen were renovating the structure's exterior on August 18, 2009, a heating gun used to remove paint mysteriously ignited and destroyed the third floor and attic of the historic home. The first and second floors were also damaged by water and smoke. Fortunately, only one item from America's largest Chinese porcelain collection was damaged. Out of the three hundred valuable pieces, only a glass pitcher from the late 1800s shattered. Also, "The Ropes Mansion at Salem, Massachussetts," Nellie S. Messer's article on the mansion, talked about fires happening in the late 1800s after Abigail Ropes died tragically.

All hell broke loose when three unmarried sisters—Mary, Sarah, and Eliza—introduced modern amenities to the house like hot and cold water. They also moved the entire structure back thirty feet from the street during renovations starting in 1893.

It's a recurring theme for "stay behinds," or spirits that don't know they're dead, to cause an uproar when their beloved space is being renovated. Ghosts, especially homebound spirits emotionally attached to their surroundings, don't like change. In fact, it's common for bizarre mishaps, from a heating-gun fire to a mysteriously falling ladder, to disrupt the renovation process of allegedly haunted locales. It would make sense for Ropes's spirit to make a postmortem plea to keep her mansion in the same condition she left it in 1839.

In 2015 the Peabody Essex Museum (PEM) reopened the mansion to visitors with an emphasis on giving a voice to the mansion's former owners. "The property has been reimagined and reinstalled to offer emotional snapshots of the Ropes family over time," said Josh Basseches, PEM's deputy director, to the *Salem News* on May 21, 2015. Michelle Moon, assistant director for adult programs, also commented in the article. "We wanted visitors to relate to the Ropes as a family," Moon explained.

Based on a recent visit to the so-called *Hocus Pocus* house, the latest renovations to the 250-year-old structure seem to have pleased the mansion's ghosts. The original furniture and antique mementos have been returned to the home. Curators also made a few updates, which included white-painted walls that deviated a bit from the home's original darker interior.

My tour guide told me that it's rare for a historic property to have access to the original furnishings. "When they first started doing renovations, they would find petticoats from the nineteenth century still hanging in the closets," she told me. Also, the museum painstakingly used the family's records—including diary entries and personal letters preserved at PEM's Phillips Library—to guide restoration.

In addition to spotlighting the Ropes family's happier times, they also paid homage to the dead. For example, archivists recreated the bedroom of Elizabeth Ropes Orne, who actually passed in her room from tuberculosis, the same disease that claimed her father, Joseph, when he was also in his early twenties. Orne's washbasin and the family's medicine chest are on display next to her restored canopy bed.

There's not much mention of "Nabby." However, she seemed at peace with the renovations during my recent visit. The only indication of a possible haunting was an extreme change in temperature when I entered the room where she was burned alive. Cold spots are a common indication of ghostly activity. Oddly, the temperature fluctuation seemed to be confined to a small area in the room that was mysteriously next to the fireplace.

After the renovations in 2015, the ghosts of the Ropes Mansion seemed to have moved outside. Reports from tour guides suggest that the Colonial Revival–style garden behind the mansion is now the house's haunted hotspot. Visitors claim to hear disembodied whispers and feel the occasional tap on the shoulder when no one is there.

One gentleman, Andy Bye, was the main gardener for fifty years, from 1931 to his passing in 1994. It's believed the energy in the garden is a residual haunting. However, it could be the reclusive

Abigail Ropes taking a rare stroll outside of the mansion she loved so much. In an attempt to communicate with the garden's visitors, it's believed that it's her ice-cold hands tapping visitors from behind and begging for recognition among the living.

WICKED PROFILE: MELISSA REYNOLDS, HOUSE OF THE SEVEN GABLES

"Honestly, that's our past. You learn from
your past and then you move on."
—Melissa Reynolds, House of the Seven Gables

Melissa Reynolds, human resources manager at the House of the Seven Gables, is surrounded by the curses of Salem's past. Her Gallows Hill home is a stone's throw from Proctor's Ledge, where historians believe the witch-trials victims were hanged in 1692. It's also where the Great Fire of 1914 initially started and ultimately leveled most of the city.

Melissa Reynolds is in the hub of Salem's cursed past. She lives around the corner from the witch-trials execution site, Proctor's Ledge. PHOTO BY SAM BALTRUSIS

"I believe in curses," Reynolds said from her second-floor office in the historic Retire Beckett House, the oldest structure on the House of the Seven Gables campus, built in 1655. "In the pagan world, if you curse someone it will come back to you threefold." Based on the Wiccan rule, the sins of one's ancestors are carried forward seven generations. Also, what you give out—both positive and negative—will come back to you.

In other words, what goes around comes around.

Reynolds, a Salemite for decades, can trace several generations of her family to the Witch City's cursed Gallows Hill neighborhood. In fact, her great-grandfather was a Ward, a prominent name with ties to two haunted structures in Salem. "I would have to do more research on my family's genealogy," Reynolds said, "but I wouldn't be surprised if my family had ties to the Ward properties in town."

As far as cursed Ward houses, one of them had a ringside seat to the horrors of the witch dungeon, and many people suspect the structure contains residual energy, or a psychic imprint, from the era. Built in 1684, the John Ward House was moved to its present site behind the Gardner-Pingree House in 1910 and was later restored by the Essex Institute. Considered a highly active paranormal site by local investigators, the Colonial-style dwelling originally faced Prison Lane, currently called St. Peter Street, and was next to the Giles Corey execution site in present-day Howard Street Cemetery. In the seventeenth century, it stood across the street from the Witch Gaol.

Some believe those accused of witchcraft were taken to the wood-frame-and-clapboard structure to be stripped and searched for "witchery marks" or skin anomalies like warts or moles before being tortured emotionally and physically with needles and a bevy of seventeenth-century torture devices. For the record, family members of those accused were tortured as well. John Proctor, while waiting to be executed, talked about the interrogation of Martha Carrier's sons, who "would not confess anything till they tied them neck and heels and the blood was ready to come out of their noses," Proctor wrote.

While local taverns were mainly used for interrogations, some historians believe the Ward house was also a regular interrogation spot because of its proximity to the witch dungeon. As far as paranormal activity, people who have been able to go inside the historic structure claim to hear disembodied screams from the past, perhaps from the victims allegedly tortured there. Investigators and visitors have snapped photos through the windows of full-bodied apparitions of what appear to be frightened spirits begging for help.

The other Ward structure, the Joshua Ward House on Washington Street, has been a favorite stop for local ghost tours for years. In fact, some guides have claimed it's one of Salem's most haunted buildings. However, after the long-vacant mansion was restored by Lark Hotels, its maritime past has been embraced after it was rebranded as "The Merchant" in 2015. Joshua Ward was a wealthy maritime trailblazer and sea captain. Originally the house had a view of the South River, but in 1830 the Front Street waterway was filled in.

When it comes to encounters with the Ward family ghosts, Reynolds doesn't have to visit the two historic and haunted structures bearing her family name. The human resources manager said her home on Proctor Street in Salem's Gallows Hill neighborhood is a hotbed of kindred spirits.

"My great-grandfather, John Ward, lived in upper Gallows Hill," Reynolds continued, adding that she lives in a home that has been passed down for generations. "In my house, we've experienced paranormal activity. Sometimes the ghosts are not very happy."

Reynolds believes the spirits of her deceased relatives watch over her. "I hear footsteps and voices sometimes," she explained. While she "gets along" with the ghosts in her home, Reynolds said the spirits have been aggressive toward her former boyfriend. They would yell, she claimed, and keep him up at night. "We ended up having to sage the house," she recalled. "We also put crosses on the doors using olive oil."

While she feels protected in her Proctor Street dwelling, Reynolds agreed that the area surrounding Proctor's Ledge has a "creepy vibe" to it. In fact, she believes that the Gallows Hill neighborhood may be cursed. "If someone was killed, the spirits in that house would probably be in a state of unrest," she said, adding that her neighborhood is, in essence, a historic crime scene. "They have unfinished business."

Based on previous interviews with historians and paranormal investigators, the Gallows Hill neighborhood may be experiencing what experts call an "aura of disaster," or an environment that triggers ghostly happenings.

Tim Maguire from the Salem Night Tour said he's heard tons of stories associated with the Gallows Hill Park area. "There have been several suicides," said Maguire. "Inexplicable stuff has happened there over the years."

Maguire alluded to reports of full-bodied apparitions and phantom voices. He also talked about a series of self-inflicted deaths. In 2008 a man was found hanged from a tree near the city's water tank. Officials said it "appeared to be a suicide at the time," adding there were no signs of foul play.

Mollie Stewart, former owner of Spellbound Tours, who has since relocated to New Orleans, encountered a presence when conducting an investigation near the "lower ledges" of Gallows

Hill. "As Mollie ventured up the hill, she at first didn't think too much of it when she heard voices," recounted Leslie Rule in *When the Ghost Screams*. "She figured it was just a few other people, out exploring. But then she spotted a hooded figure. As she stared, it vanished before her eyes."

Based on ghost lore, hauntings have been associated with the lack of proper burial or a later desecration of the grave. Countless spirits, according to paranormal researchers, have been traced to missing gravestones or vandalism of a resting place. Perhaps the spirits reported wandering the Gallows Hill area are making a postmortem plea for a proper burial?

Historians believe the bodies of at least a dozen of the witch-trials victims were thrown in a shallow ditch or the rocky crevices of Proctor's Ledge.

As far as the history of Gallows Hill Park, the city acquired the site in 1912. The issue surrounding the exact location of where the hangings took place resurfaced in 1998 when the city announced plans to build a school at what was believed to be the execution site. "There has been, for at least ninety years, a link in the community between the hangings and that site," said Liz Griffin in the March 23, 1998, edition of the *Salem Evening News*. "When the city—back in the late 1800s—started looking at that land, the original purpose was to buy a small piece of that land to put up a monument to commemorate the tragedy."

Salem's city council set aside money in the 1890s to buy "witch square" on Gallows Hill, a spot near the top of the park where people originally believed the hangings took place. However, one local historian, Marilynne Roach, challenged the historically accepted spot in 1997, claiming that the nineteen men and women killed in 1692—excluding Giles Corey, who was pressed to death—most likely were hanged on the "lower ledges" of Gallows Hill or the public wooded land between Proctor and Pope Streets.

Roach, coupled with a team of scholars from a group called the Gallows Hill Project, pinpointed the exact location using evidence from court notes dating back to August 1692. Rebecca Eames, a woman suspected of witchcraft who was taken from her home in Boxford, said she saw the gallows from Boston Street while on her way to downtown Salem.

After exhaustive research, the group of historians came to an agreement in early January 2016 that the execution site was located behind the Walgreens at 59 Boston Street. A crescent-shaped granite memorial was erected in 2017, honoring the 325-year anniversary of when five of the innocent women were hanged for witchcraft on July 19, 1692.

The recently pinpointed gallows, Proctor's Ledge, is literally around the corner from Melissa Reynolds's house. However, she believes that the memorial doesn't necessarily mark the correct spot.

"Where they have the monument isn't exactly where it should be. It's higher up," she told me. "The Proctor's Ledge location is private property. I personally think it would be nice to have a memorial where they were actually killed. But there's not much they could do because it's residential."

When asked if she believes that the nineteen hangings in 1692 are somehow related to the restless spirits in her home, Reynolds shrugged. Who knows? "Honestly, that's our past," she said. "You learn from your past and then you move on."

Cotton Mather

While Salem's series of hearings and prosecutions in 1692 continues to cast a spell on the masses, Cambridge and Boston were bit by the mob malady as well, and many of the same finger pointers, including the Reverend Cotton Mather, perpetuated a similar frenzy in small villages throughout New England's blood-soaked landscape.

Witch hunts? Yep, Boston and Cambridge had them too.

The Newtowne Market jail in present-day Harvard Square was built between Winthrop Square and Eliot Street (currently home to Staples and the Park restaurant) in 1692, when the witch-hunt mentality started to sweep New England. Many women who were accused of cavorting with evil and Quakers like Anne Hutchinson were imprisoned there but never hanged. Some, like Lydia Dustin, who was declared not guilty of the dark arts but couldn't afford the prison fees, died tragically in shackles. In contrast, Dustin's relative Elizabeth Coleson was also accused and found not guilty of so-called evil. She was released several days before her grandmother's tragic death on March 10, 1693.

Boston's alleged witches, like Ann "Goody" Glover, weren't as lucky. Glover, a self-sufficient, strong-willed Irishwoman who spoke fluent Gaelic, lived in the North End, where she washed laundry for John Goodwin and his family. After a spirited spat in her native Gaelic tongue with Goodwin's thirteen-year-old daughter, Martha, Glover was accused of bewitching the four children in the household and was sent to prison for practicing the dark arts.

Reverend Mather, who later became a player in Salem's trials, wrote in his book *Memorable Providences* that Glover was a "scandalous old Irish woman, very poor, a Roman Catholic and obstinate in idolatry." During her trial, Glover was asked to recite the Lord's Prayer. Speaking in broken English, she only knew the Catholic, rather than the Puritan Protestant, version of the prayer. She was hanged in Boston's gallows on November 16, 1688. Glover was one of four women who were accused, and executed, for witchcraft in Boston over a forty-year period beginning with the execution of Margaret Jones in 1648.

"I would be hesitant to say that Boston and Cambridge were more progressive back then," said historian Gavin W. Kleespies. "You have people like Cotton Mather coming out of Cambridge and then heading off to Salem during the witch hysteria. His father, Increase Mather, was a Puritan leader and administrator at Harvard. Cotton accused innocent people of witchcraft and then sent them to prison, and some of them were held in Cambridge."

Apparently, "the prison was atrocious" in Cambridge and housed many women, including Goody Elizabeth Kendall, who were wrongly accused of witchcraft. Kendall was believed to be executed at Gallows Hill, in North Cambridge, during the seventeenth-century hysteria.

Kleespies, a Cambridge native who returned to his hometown in 2008 after earning a master's degree at the University of Chicago, said the city didn't become a center for progressive thought until the late eighteenth century. "Puritan New England was horrifying in many ways," he continued. "I wouldn't say there was a blood lust, but there was definitely a callousness back then."

As far as Cotton's role in the Salem witch trials, there is no doubt that the young reverend "acted as puppeteer and almost single-handedly heated the crucible that would explode into a small-scale massacre," wrote Lauren Grobaty in the *Harvard Crimson*. "He used his family's political clout to ensure that William Stoughton, a staunch man of God, was appointed chief justice, a position that involved presiding over a special witchcraft tribunal."

Cotton, a Harvard student at eleven years old, also suggested that "spectral evidence," or made-up testimony that a spirit could testify against an accused victim or even attack the afflicted girls, should be permitted in the trials. However, the family's tune changed once the politically powerful father stepped in and rallied against his son's propaganda.

While Cotton wrote that he didn't attend the trials in Salem, author Robert Calef said that he most certainly did. Calef, author of the defamatory *More Wonders of the Invisible World,* claimed that Mather was present at the execution of the Reverend George Burroughs. After Calef's book was published, local lore suggests that Increase orchestrated a burning of the book in Harvard Yard and, in a public act of defiance to protect his son's reputation, was removed as the college's seventh president.

However, it didn't work. In fact, some people believe that the younger Mather was cursed. Cotton never became a political powerhouse like his father. He ended up losing his wife and three children during a measles outbreak in 1713. Cotton Mather passed in 1728 and was buried with his father at Copp's Hill Cemetery in Boston's North End.

COTTON MATHER'S HAUNT: BOSTON'S NORTH END

Based purely on aesthetic, Boston's North End should be haunted. In fact, horror writer H. P. Lovecraft believed the neighborhood was fertile ground for the supernatural. In *Pickman's Model*, the author convincingly wrote about the inexplicable magic of the North End's spirited underbelly, adding that "the whole North End once had a set of tunnels that kept certain people in touch with each other's houses, and the burying ground and the sea." He also talked about the lack of ghosts in Boston's Back Bay, saying the newly created land around Newbury Street hasn't been around long enough "to pick up memories and attract local spirits."

The Reverend Cotton Mather, along with his influential family members, including his Harvard president father Increase, is buried in the Mather Tomb in Copp's Hill Cemetery in the North End. "The second-oldest cemetery in Boston, Copp's Hill was established in 1659 and is filled with famous figures such as Cotton and Increase Mather, as well as former slaves and revolutionary soldiers," reported the website OnlyInYourState. "Some say the hallowed ground is haunted by the spirit of Increase Mather, a fierce and imposing colonial preacher who condemned many of the so-called Salem witches to hell."

While the blogger probably mixed up the Harvard president with his witch-hunting son, the legend associated with the lingering spirit at Copp's Hill suggests it's the Reverend Cotton Mather and not his dad, Increase. "Some visitors see glowing orbs of light appear amongst the tombstones, while others say they have felt unseen bodies brush against them in the dark," the website claimed.

Is Copp's Hill Cemetery haunted by Cotton? It's possible. However, locals in the North End notoriously remain tight-lipped about the neighborhood's ghost lore.

Michael Baker, head of the group called the New England Center for the Advancement of Paranormal Science (NECAPS) and member of Para-Boston, leaves no gravestone unturned when he investigates a so-called haunted location, which includes a few of the old structures in the North End. Baker said he's heard very few reports of ghosts in the historic buildings surrounding Copp's Hill Cemetery. Why? He believes it's a cultural thing.

"The North End seems a bit devoid of claims," Baker said when asked about the lack of alleged paranormal activity in the historically Italian neighborhood. "I have always felt much of it has to do with the religious views of the people who live there. There are a lot of old-school Italian families there, people who tend to be well embedded in religious culture. I have noticed that this old-world approach to religion often brings with it an unspoken rule about dabbling in or acknowledging things related to the paranormal."

Oddly, one of Boston's more infamous made-up ghost stories involves a man leaving his Middle Street home in the North End. William Austin's Peter Rugg literary character—who stubbornly rode his horse into a thunderstorm in 1770 and was cursed to drive his carriage until the end of time—was completely fabricated. However, people over the years have reportedly spotted the ghostly man with his daughter by his side frantically trying to make the trek back to Boston.

According to the legend, Rugg was visiting Concord with his daughter and stopped by a tavern recommended to him by a longtime friend before heading back to Boston. A violent thunderstorm was heading in their direction, and the watering hole's owner insisted that Rugg and his daughter stay the night. Rugg, a notoriously defiant old man, refused the offer and headed directly into the storm. The horse and its driver never returned to Boston. However, people claimed to have seen what was called "the Stormbreeder," a phantom carriage driven by Rugg and considered to be the precursor to a thunderstorm, all over New England. One man in Connecticut said he had a face-to-face encounter with the ghost. "I have lost the road to Boston. My name is Peter Rugg," the specter supposedly said before vanishing into thin air.

For many, the only real ghosts that exist are the ones that haunt the insides of their heads.

"There are some claims in the North End," continued Baker. "I know there are stories about the tunnels there. I have had a few calls from the North End over the years, but unfortunately they never amounted to anything significant."

Baker isn't ruling out the possibility of ghosts in the North End. However, he hasn't found anything substantial while investigating there and finds the locals to be unusually tight-lipped. "I know several old Italian families and they won't even embrace a discussion about ghosts," he said. "To them it's religiously forbidden. Of course, this is just my speculation, but it's a pattern I've seen in people I speak with."

While the North End is mysteriously devoid of reported ghost sightings, the legends associated with its series of rumored underground tunnels seem to be based on reported fact. "There definitely were tunnels underneath the North End," explained Peter Muise, author of *Legends and Lore of the North Shore*. "For example, in the nineteenth century construction workers discovered that a house at 453 Commercial Street had an archway in its cellar that connected to a large tunnel. It led from Commercial Street up toward Salem Street. Unfortunately this house was demolished in 1906 and the tunnel entrance along with it."

Who built the tunnels? Muise said they were probably built in the 1700s by Thomas Gruchy, a privateer who became wealthy from raiding Spanish ships. "He invested his loot in several Boston businesses, including a distillery, a warehouse, and several wharves. His wealth was excessive even for a privateer, and many of his neighbors suspected that he was somehow smuggling goods into Boston without having to pay the British tariffs. Despite his shady background, he became a prominent member of Boston society. He purchased the Salem Street mansion of former governor Phips in 1745, threw lavish parties, and became a congregant at the Old North Church. Four plaster angels that he looted from a French ship still decorate the church today."

Gruchy mysteriously disappeared in 1759 and left behind a legacy of underground tunnels and stolen goods. "At the height of his wealth and popularity, Gruchy vanished from Boston and was never seen again," Muise explained. "It's believed that he was smuggling goods past the British using a series of underground tunnels, and fled town when they discovered what he was doing. Sadly his mansion on Salem Street was torn down years ago."

Muise said that many secrets are buried beneath the North End's blood-stained soil. "A few other North End tunnels have been found," he said. "A book from 1817 mentions a tunnel under a house on Lynn Street, and a guide to Boston architecture notes that the cellar of a house on Salem Street still has an entrance to a tunnel in its basement. It has been bricked off, so it's not clear where the tunnel goes or what it was used for."

Could the ghosts of the North End be hiding in these hidden tunnels? Yes, it's possible that they're lurking in the shadows beneath the cobblestone streets traveled by thousands of tourists flocking to a neighborhood famous for its old-school Italian eateries, Paul Revere, and the Mather family's tomb.

Elias Hasket Derby

There's no denying that Salem's native son Nathaniel Hawthorne left his imprint on the city. In the introductory chapter of his famous novel of betrayal, *The Scarlet Letter*, Hawthorne described finding the scarlet *A* that inspired his tale in a spare room of the Custom House when he worked there as a surveyor between 1846 and 1849.

Hawthorne was evasive when journalists asked him to produce the famous scarlet *A* and later said one of his children dropped the infamous red letter into a fire.

Whether Hawthorne's tale was true or not, the Custom House, which was built in 1819, continues to be a hot spot for tourists visiting Salem. A carved wooden bald eagle, painted gold, sits atop the Custom House, alluding to the historic building's heyday in the early 1800s, when custom duties, not income taxes, were the primary source of government revenue.

An oil painting of Elias Hasket Derby Sr., the country's first millionaire, hangs above the desk where Hawthorne worked. His view from the office space is the historic Derby Wharf, which was extended to its current length of more than one mile in 1806. Work on the wharf was started in 1762 by its wealthy namesake.

Both the Custom House and the Derby Wharf are allegedly teeming with the spirits of Salem's maritime past, ranging from ghostly pirates mysteriously emerging from the water and walking around to salty sea captains whispering in the Custom House about their treasures smuggled in from overseas.

Shipbuilding flourished in Salem. By 1750 the city's commerce was enmeshed with the sea, and brazen sea captains sailed their ships to the West Indies and traded lumber and fish for sugar and molasses. During the Revolutionary War, Salem was the country's primary seaport because the British had barricaded Boston and New York. By 1820, with the exception of the embargo during the War of 1812, Salem was flourishing and fast-sailing ships were built for trade with China and India. Pepper and spices were brought back and sold for an enormous profit.

There was also a lot of seediness going on during this era, and many of the ghosts supposedly haunting the Custom House and Derby Wharf are tied to the darker side of Salem's golden maritime era.

Pirates? Yep, Salem had them. However, they were given a less disparaging title. They were called "privateers." Of course, the Derby Wharf area has a few pirate ghosts looking for their long-lost booty.

So, how did the so-called privateers smuggle the goods past the custom agents? One theory is that Elias Hasket Derby's son built a series of underground tunnels in 1801 connecting the wharf and various homes and buildings scattered throughout downtown Salem. Christopher Dowgin, author of *Salem Secret Underground*, weaved together a convincing history of the city's tunnels. "From the various wharfs, goods were smuggled through trap doors into the tunnels that led to the merchants' and ship captains' homes," Dowgin wrote. "There the goods were stored till they moved them to their stores on Essex Street."

Speaking of the tunnels, many believe these secret underground passageways are haunted. Dowgin talked about one spooky incident near Blaney Street. "I just barely lifted my cell phone from its case on my belt when the phone flew twenty-five feet into an open manhole," he commented, adding that the batteries of electronic devices mysteriously drain and orbs show up regularly in photos near the wharf.

Visitors who are sensitive to the paranormal often report seeing full-bodied apparitions of salty seafarers walking aimlessly around Derby Wharf. Others claim to have heard footsteps when no one is there. Cold spots on warm summer days, an indication of paranormal activity, are the norm near the lighthouse at the end of the wharf. One woman felt an icy tap on her shoulder and spotted what looked like an 1800s-era fisherman, who immediately disappeared when she turned around.

The scene inside the Custom House is said to be equally active. While tour guides are notoriously tight-lipped about the structure's supposed hauntings, visitors have heard disembodied footsteps echo throughout the brick Federal-style building. There are also reports of inexplicable flickering lights emanating from within the Custom House that disappear when people approach them.

So, did Hawthorne believe the Custom House was haunted? Probably not.

Several writers opined that the *Scarlet Letter* writer was creeped out by the building's spirits. "Maybe Hawthorne knew a bit more about the place than he let on," wrote Thomas D'Agostino in *A Guide to Haunted New England*. Based on historical research, there's no concrete proof he had a close encounter there. In fact, during his stint at the Custom House, the author expressed more skepticism than belief in the existence of paranormal activity. However, he did write about spirits in his books, specifically *The House of the Seven Gables,* later in his career.

ELIAS HASKET DERBY'S HAUNT: OLD TOWN HALL

Opened in 1816 and used as headquarters for the city's government until 1837, Salem's Old Town Hall is known for its ghostly inhabitants wearing period garb. I've heard all sorts of reports about supposed activity at the location, including large items like chairs and doors moving on their own. People also claim to have seen outlines of men and women appearing in the windows at night when the building is closed and empty.

On one of my tours, a woman from California flipped out when I spoke in front of Old Town Hall. Home to the reenactment of Bridget Bishop's trial, called *Cry Innocent,* the historic structure is famous for the dance sequence in the movie *Hocus Pocus.* It's also where I launched my third book, *Ghosts of Salem: Haunts of the Witch City,* and later shared a vendor table with my fellow ghost writer, Joni Mayhan, at the paranormal convention called Salem Con. The out-of-town visitor on my tour swore she saw two ghostly faces pressed against the window on the second floor of Town Hall, as if they were intently listening to what I said.

Before it was Town Hall, there was a mansion on the property for Salem's first millionaire, Elias Hasket Derby. He had the beautiful house constructed at the height of his wealth. His wife, Elizabeth Crowninshield, moved in with him and they both ended up dying from pneumonia because the mansion was so drafty. Because of the expenses related to its upkeep, Derby's heirs tore down the structure, known as the "Versailles of Salem," soon after the patriarch's death on September 8, 1799.

People have seen a couple dancing through the windows at night, and I strongly believe it's Derby and his wife waltzing in the afterlife.

As far as the pirate ghosts spotted at the cursed millionaire's namesake, Derby Wharf, one theory is that they're residual hauntings, or a videotape replay of the maritime action back in the early 1800s.

Another possibility could be related to a tragedy involving a deadly close encounter at sea on March 6, 1869. During a torrential storm that eventually became a hurricane, a Salem-based schooner known as the *Andrew Johnson* had a fatal collision with a so-called hoodoo ship named the *Charles Haskell*. Apparently, the *Haskell* had a history of bad luck. In fact, one workman slipped on board and broke his neck. Also, its first captain quit before the ship's maiden voyage because he believed the vessel was cursed.

According to accounts from the *Haskell*, the schooner rammed into the *Andrew Johnson* during the hurricane and ripped it into pieces. The *Johnson* was literally sliced open. The surviving ship's crew witnessed their peers frantically trying to stay alive as the vessel and its ten men were engulfed by the thrashing sea.

One legend gives an alternative to the spirits haunting Derby Wharf. According to the book *Weird Massachusetts*, the night watchmen on the *Haskell* encountered similar phantoms on board several days after they witnessed the *Johnson* sink into its watery grave.

"They saw dark, shadowy figures rising out of the sea," wrote Jeff Belanger. "There were ten of them in all, and as they reached the *Haskell* the watchmen could see that the figures looked like men. The dark wraiths reached their hands over the rail of the schooner and climbed aboard. Their eyes were black, like hollowed-out holes, and they wore dark and oily sealskins for clothes. The phantoms quickly took up positions around the ship and began to go through the motions of casting lines, rigging sails and setting the anchor."

Perhaps the ghostly seafarers regularly spotted on Derby Wharf are the casualties of the ill-fated *Andrew Johnson*. It's said that the crew was never to be seen or heard from again—at least, not among the living. Maybe the men have finally made it home after being lost at sea for almost 150 years.

George Corwin

If there was one easy-to-finger villain from the Salem witch trials, it would probably be high sheriff George Corwin. Although it was his uncle, Jonathan Corwin, who tried and accused the innocents along with John Hathorne as magistrates of the Court of Oyer and Terminer, the sheriff was responsible for carrying out their orders. And boy, did he.

Corwin's enforcement of the sentences served up by the court was downright cruel, based on original documents and personal accounts. He would confiscate items from the families of the innocents days after they were executed. Corwin was known to be particularly sadistic during the execution of Giles Corey, the elderly landowner who was pressed to death. Based on one passed-down legend, the sheriff used the tip of his walking stick to push Corey's tongue back into his mouth as he fought to breathe during the particularly gruesome death by pressing, or peine forte et dure.

Another more dramatic account claimed that Corwin tried to squeeze a confession out of Corey. "Do you confess?" demanded Corwin, as his men piled more rocks on the stubborn landowner. Corwin reportedly would stand on top of the rocks as the old man demanded "more weight."

According to legend perpetuated by Robert Calef's *More Wonders of the Invisible World,* Corey cursed the sheriff and Salem right before he passed.

Based on what unfolded in the years after the trials, it's possible that Corey's alleged hex actually worked. Corwin was in his twenties during the witch trials but mysteriously had a heart attack when he turned thirty. It's said that when Corwin died in 1696, he was a wanted man.

Although the Supreme Court ruled in 1694 that he was following orders when he confiscated goods during the witch-trials hysteria, Corwin was repeatedly sued by Philip English, a wealthy merchant who fled Salem to Boston and ultimately New York with his wife, Mary. If Corey actually cursed Corwin, then it was English who was responsible for carrying it out. Four years after the witch trials, English supposedly threatened to place a lien on Corwin's corpse until his property was returned.

Originally from the British Channel Islands, English owned a fleet of twenty-one ships, several buildings throughout town, and a palatial mansion on Essex Street. He was arguably the richest man in Salem as of 1686, which is probably why he and his wife were accused of practicing the dark arts during the hysteria six years later.

On Saturday, April 18, Corwin and his cronies served a warrant for the arrest of English's wife, Mary. The following day, Corwin brought her to the Cat and Wheel, a tavern near the old meetinghouse, and she was locked in a room on the second floor. Examinations of supposed witches were held at Salem's taverns, so it's no surprise that the local watering hole was used as a more-humane holding cell compared to the hell-on-Earth dungeon located near Federal Street. Philip was heartbroken and would visit his wife three times a day.

While Mary was being held prisoner, one of the afflicted girls, Susannah Sheldon, accused Mary's husband of being a witch. She said English "stepped over his pew and pinched her" during a church service on Sunday, April 24, "in a very sad manner." Sheldon also claimed that English brought her the devil's book and forced her to sign it or he would cut her throat. Weeks earlier, Sheldon had claimed to have seen Mary's apparition alongside a dark man with a tall hat.

Because of his social status, Philip English was sent to Boston. While he was held captive in the neighboring city's more relaxed prison, he arranged for his wife to join him. During their stay in the state's cultural hub, which involved supervised overnight lockdowns, they attended a service at the First Church in Boston. During the sermon, the ministers read Matthew 10:23: "When they persecute you in one town, flee to another." English listened. The unfortunate couple maneuvered a prison break and fled to New York in a carriage donated by one of their friends.

During the witch-trials hysteria, food was scarce in Salem because of a drought, and English, who learned about the horrors happening back home, sent a ship full of corn to feed the suffering. The couple returned to Salem in May 1693 after the governor of Massachusetts, Sir William Phips, issued a general pardon of the remaining accused witches. The Englishes were free, even though they were traumatized by the capricious ordeal.

According to lore, English held a lifelong resentment against sheriff George Corwin, who had ransacked his palatial Salem estate on Essex Street, confiscating up to 1,500 pounds sterling. After returning to the Witch City, English's wife died during childbirth in 1694, and Philip passed forty-two years later, still suffering from lingering resentment and seeking revenge on the sheriff who destroyed his property.

Corwin was buried beneath his home, at the current location of the Joshua Ward House at 148 Washington Street—presently a boutique hotel called the Merchant—and was later moved when tempers cooled to the Broad Street Cemetery with his equally disliked uncle, Judge Jonathan Corwin.

GEORGE CORWIN'S HAUNT: BROAD STREET CEMETERY

As far as haunted cemeteries in Salem, the second-oldest burial ground in the city is often overlooked. Because of its relative seclusion on Lawes Hill, a small mound bordered by Summer, Broad, and Gedney Streets, this picturesque cemetery located a mere stone's throw from the allegedly haunted Salem Inn and the Witch House is rarely visited by the living. But it's apparently a hot spot for the dead.

Why? Broad Street Cemetery was established in 1655 and is the final resting place for Court of Oyer and Terminer judge Jonathan Corwin, as well as Salem's more infamous player from the 1692 witch-trials era, Corwin's nephew and high sheriff George Corwin.

As far as hauntings, the younger Corwin's final resting place is said to be a lesser-known hotbed of paranormal activity. Floating orbs of light, an indicator of high levels of residual psychic energy, have been spotted in the cemetery. There have also been several reports of an apparition of an older gentleman wearing period garb wandering the old-school gravestones.

One spirited encounter from 1975 indicates that the Broad Street Cemetery ghost is a whistler. "All of sudden, a glimmer of white caught my eyes," recalled one visitor interviewed by the *Boston Globe* in October 1975. "There, on a grave to the right, was a man's shoulder, the shadow of his head was turning, and out from his mouth came a jagged, high-pitched whistling sound." The freaked-out witness continued, "Something that night didn't want us around Salem. Driving away, we believed that it was Corwin, warning us to leave, not to deal in forces and intrigues we were just novices at."

Is it Sheriff Corwin's spirit? Perhaps. However, the descriptions of the garb of the "whistling man" spirit seem to date back to the eighteenth century. Also, Corwin's spirit is rumored to linger at his former homestead, the land currently occupied by the Joshua Ward House. Meanwhile, it's said that the residual energy of Corwin's uncle supposedly left its imprint at the nearby Witch House.

One theory suggests that the whistling specter isn't a Corwin but a man named Jonathan Neal.

Broad Street Cemetery is directly across from Salem's picturesque Chestnut Street neighborhood, which continues to be a hub of photo-seeking tourists. The Jonathan Neal House, originally thought to have been built by its namesake in 1767, is now believed to date back to 1652 thanks to the discovery of a deed proving the conversion of a barn on the property forty years before the Salem witch-trials hysteria. Oddly, Neal suffered a freakish death in 1790. The carpenter from Marblehead and grandson of early settler John Neal ran a local waterfront warehouse and, after drinking a few too many in a "house of intemperance," fell head first into the mud and died tragically.

Based on the research of famed paranormal investigators like the late, great Dr. Hans Holzer, it's common for spirits who have died accidentally while intoxicated to stick around. Some believe Neal may be what is known as a "stay behind" who lingers in the area surrounding Broad Street Cemetery near his home. Holzer, in an interview in 2005, explained the phenomenon. "'Stay behinds' are relatively common," he said. "Somebody dies, and then they're really surprised that all of a sudden they're not dead. They're alive like they were. They don't understand it because they weren't prepared for it. So they go back to what they knew most—their chair, their room, and they just sit there. Next, they want to let people know that they're still 'alive.' So they'll do little things like moving things, appear to relatives, pushing objects, poltergeist phenomena, and so on."

The odd thing about Neal is that he was known to whistle and was possibly doing so when he fell face first in the mud that freakishly killed him. Spine-chilling whistles from the afterlife? Yep, it's an attribute of one of the many spirits of Salem hanging out in its historic cemeteries.

Harry Houdini

Escape artist and magician Harry Houdini had more than a few tricks up his sleeve. In fact, when he visited Salem in 1906, he staged an impressive preshow tease at the former jail at 15 Front Street. Slotted to perform at the Salem Theatre during a three-day gig, Houdini orchestrated a well-publicized stunt challenging the local police to handcuff and then shackle him at the jail.

While he defied local police in other cities during his tour throughout New England, Houdini managed to wow the Witch City with a well-publicized twist. In Salem, he did it naked.

"Houdini released himself from three pairs of police handcuffs and two pairs of leg irons, got out of one cell and into another, where every stitch of his clothing had been locked," reported the *Salem Evening News* on April 17, 1906. He then "opened a third cell and shackled himself to a prisoner, unlocked the outside door and walked around to the city marshal's office all in thirteen minutes by the watch."

Yes, the master showman was completely naked and then managed to retrieve his clothing before chaining himself to a prisoner. He even met the impossible challenge under fifteen minutes. Of course, his sold-out engagements at the Salem Theatre didn't disappoint.

The description alone in the newspaper was entertaining. "His arms, both hands being covered with the long closed sleeves, were lashed tightly around him and the ropes tied with a dozen or more knots behind his back and a stout leather strap buckled around his neck," recounted the *Salem Evening News*. "Houdini threw himself upon the floor, squirmed and struggled, dislocated his shoulders so that his hands were above his head."

There is no doubt that he left an indelible imprint on Salem. However, the escapologist probably wouldn't be thrilled with the dozens of card readers with shops on Essex Street. Houdini spent most of the 1920s debunking psychics and mediums. He would even attend séances in disguise in an attempt to discredit them.

Houdini died tragically on October 31, 1926, in Detroit, Michigan. While the actual circumstances involving his demise have been associated with the extreme Water-Torture Cell escape at the Garrick Theatre and even a subversive plot by the spiritualists to stop him, he ultimately died from several punches to his abdomen, which ruptured his appendix.

According to legend, he told his wife, Bess, that he would try to contact her in the afterlife. Before his death, the couple supposedly agreed on a secret phrase, "Rosabelle, believe," alluding to a song Bess performed during their courtship. She would sit in a dark room, beneath a portrait of Houdini, waiting for him to message her from beyond. His spirit never came.

While Bess eventually gave up, the séances continued and eventually ended up in Salem at the Hawthorne Hotel on the anniversary of Houdini's death in 1990, which happens to be Halloween. The event attracted hundreds of thrill-seekers hoping to connect with the cursed icon. Led by a self-proclaimed psychic, Robert Steiner, the group tried to summon the spirit of the escape artist in the Hawthorne Hotel's ballroom. "Are you there, Harry Houdini? Can you hear us? Please speak to us. Please give us a sign," said Steiner in a report by the *Salem Evening News.* "No ghostly voices were heard. No furniture levitated. No unearthly winds blew through the ballroom," the article continued.

Even though the organizers claimed that they had high hopes that the Salem séance would be a success, they sheepishly told reporters that the experiment failed. It could have been the fact that they hired a psychic from the West Coast, they joked, and Steiner somehow gave Houdini the wrong directions. The organizers allegedly couldn't find a psychic in Salem to lead the evocation, even though there were several very talented clairvoyants in the room that night.

For the record, Steiner wrote a book in 1989 called *Don't Get Taken.* He notoriously used techniques to fool people into thinking he was actually a psychic. So, it was all a sham. Of course, the large crowd gathered at the Hawthorne Hotel wasn't amused.

The front-page headline of the following day's *Salem Evening News* article read: "Harry Houdini Snubs Slick Salem Séance."

HARRY HOUDINI'S HAUNT: HAWTHORNE HOTEL

When it comes to hotels replete with paranormal residue, Salem is a hotbed of paranormal activity. "The Hawthorne Hotel is built on a property that once held a building that burned down six times taking many lives," wrote Christopher Dowgin on *Salem Secret Underground*'s blog. "In its parking lot once stood the

Crowninshield-Bentley House, which was featured in H. P. Lovecraft's *Thing on the Doorstep*. Its other parking lot is holy ground for a Jewish Temple that once stood there."

As far as hauntings are concerned, the Hawthorne Hotel allegedly boasts phantom hands in Room 325 and a full-bodied female apparition on the sixth floor. However, when Syfy's *Ghost Hunters* investigated reports in 2007 of strange sounds like children crying and unseen forces touching guests in the hotel, the crew didn't uncover anything supernatural. Yet enthusiasts continue to claim a female apparition hovers in front of Room 612.

Based on a recent investigation with Amy Bruni's Strange Escapes group, I can say without hesitation that the Hawthorne Hotel's haunted suite on the sixth floor is in fact haunted. Bruni, formerly a longtime investigator on *Ghost Hunters* and currently with *Kindred Spirits*, asked me to give tours of Salem and the Hawthorne Hotel before her group headed to Bermuda on a cruise ship. I asked my psychic friend Colleen F. Costello, who recently appeared on *Paranormal Lockdown* with Nick Groff and has worked with Bruni in the past, to help me.

"There was so much electricity that night," Costello remembered. "When we took the haunted elevator to the sixth floor, everybody on the tour said they felt like they were standing on a boat. It felt like waves. We were surrounded by spirit energy in Room 612."

When Costello and I entered the haunted suite, we both heard a distinct voice demanding that we get out of the room. After that initial encounter, I decided it was in my best interest to spend as little time as possible in the haunted suite. I also invited my friend Rachel Hoffman from Paranormal Xpeditions to help with the investigation while Costello and I gave walking tours throughout Salem. Thankfully, Hoffman led the investigations for the remainder of the night.

Salem's most active? The Hawthorne Hotel continues to make national "haunted hotel" lists, even though the team from *Ghost Hunters* didn't capture paranormal activity during its made-for-TV investigation.

History and mystery ooze from the lobby of the Hawthorne Hotel, which opened its gilded doors on July 23, 1925, amid much fanfare and excitement. Approximately 1,110 of the area's residents and businessmen bought stock in what would become the city's grande dame: a six-story, 150-room hotel on a piece of land formerly occupied by the fire-prone Franklin Building.

Yes, the Hawthorne Hotel site had a history of bad luck, which included a series of destructive fires. "An easterly gale was raging, and the fire progressed, in spite of all of the efforts to save it, until the noble structure, which has been one of our institutions for about sixty years, and which extended from Essex to Forrester street, was a complete mess of ruins," reported the *Salem Register.*

Of course, the building named after Salem's native son Nathaniel Hawthorne has been plagued by less-destructive blazes over the years. In October 1997 a small fire broke out in the hotel's basement and caused an estimated $10,000 in damage. "Smoke reached all six floors of the hotel, and the Hawthorne's main ballroom suffered considerable smoke damage," reported the *Salem Evening News.* Luckily, no one was hurt.

It's possible that the psychic imprint from the cursed land's past may have caused what parapsychologists call an aura of disaster—fertile ground for the birthing of ghosts. According to several accounts over the years, the Hawthorne Hotel does indeed have a storied history of alleged paranormal activity.

"Surrounded by the many grand homes erected by the wealthy sea captains, the Salem Marine Society was founded by the skippers in 1766," wrote Lynda Lee Macken in *Haunted Salem & Beyond*. "The society's building was razed when the town determined it was time to construct the hotel. As a condition of acquiring the land, the hotel's owners agreed to provide a meeting place for the men. Some employees wonder if the spirits of some of those old sea captains have returned."

The Salem Marine Society's secret meeting spot is on the off-limits roof of the Hawthorne Hotel and is an exact replica of a cabin from the *Taria Topan*, one of the last Salem vessels to sail regularly during its golden maritime trips to East India. Several employees and visitors claim that the large ship wheel now in the restaurant mysteriously spins, as if unseen hands are steering it, when no one is there.

Other encounters include water faucets turning on and off and toilets flushing on their own. There have been many reports of disembodied voices echoing throughout the hotel and so-called phantom hands in the structure's allegedly most-active rooms, 325 and 612.

When the TV show *Bewitched* shot several episodes in Salem, the cast and crew used the allegedly haunted Hawthorne Hotel as their home base. In fact, Elizabeth Montgomery's stay in Salem is immortalized in a Samantha Stephens statue in Lappin Park. For those out of the pop-culture loop, Montgomery rode into town to film eight episodes of *Bewitched* during the summer of 1970.

"For years after the two episodes aired as the *Salem Saga*, the hotel desk fielded telephone calls asking if this was the Hawthorne Hotel that was seen on *Bewitched*," reported the hotel's newsletter. In the show, the building was known as the Hawthorne Motor Hotel.

The elevator made famous during its *Bewitched* days apparently has a mind of its own. It's believed to be haunted by an invisible presence, and some say a ghostly woman has taken a ride with them in the elevator. The same female residual haunting has been spotted in rooms and mysteriously disappears when guests confront her.

The Hawthorne Hotel's reputation as Salem's "most haunted" sometimes surpasses its historical significance. In 2007 it made the fourth slot on Travelocity's haunted hotel list, which surveyed overnight haunts across the country.

However, the hotel's general manager said the claims of paranormal activity simply weren't true. In fact, she cited the episode of *Ghost Hunters* shot at the hotel as proof. "There's no documentation," said Juli Lederhaus in the October 24, 2011, report in the *Boston Globe*. "People tell us they feel things, whatever, but we don't have any documentation. Of course, [guests] do look up haunted hotels on the Internet, and those things pop up. The more people cite those kinds of stories, the more they get published out there. I feel like I'm constantly putting out fires."

Oddly, fire may be the "psychic residue" visitors claim to sense when visiting the hotel.

Lederhaus reiterated that the myth—which is perpetuated in several books—that the hotel marks the former site of Bridget Bishop's apple orchard just isn't true. For the record, Bishop's property was near the current spot of the old Lyceum Hall. Investigators with *Ghost Hunters* told the general manager that they had visited the library and City Hall and conducted research on the physical property and had found that "nothing happened at the hotel that would cause hauntings," she claimed.

Seriously? The TV researchers completely overlooked the six fires that plagued the land's previous occupant, the Franklin Building, during the 1800s. "A few years since, a brick partition wall was erected, and this saved the entire building from destruction and prevented the conflagration from spreading to an untold extent among the wooden structures in the vicinity," reported the *Daily Advertiser* on February 1, 1845.

John Marsicano, a regular visitor to the hotel, said the *Ghost Hunters* investigation shouldn't rule out the possibility of paranormal activity. "I think those guys are good and do their endeavor earnestly and are honest about it," he told the *Globe*. "But ghosts and spirits, if they do anything, might not do it on command."

Of course, Lederhaus did point out that two other buildings existed at the site before the hotel. "Could something have happened in one of those buildings?" she said. "Who knows?"

Nathaniel Hawthorne

Salem-bred Nathaniel Hawthorne, author of *The Scarlet Letter* and *The House of the Seven Gables*, had a love-hate relationship with his hometown. Even though he spent the majority of his youth in the North Shore city, Hawthorne mused that he was "invariably happier elsewhere."

In fact, he and his family moved to a remote cottage in western Massachusetts after he was fired following a three-year stint as a surveyor at Salem's Custom House. After writing what is viewed as a negative depiction of Salem in the introduction to *The Scarlet Letter*, he traveled throughout the Boston area, returning to Salem only a handful of times in the last fourteen years of his life.

While the resentment toward his hometown lingered to his death in 1864, there's no denying that Hawthorne and his family left an indelible imprint on the city. In fact, his ancestor was John Hathorne, a witch-trials magistrate who was later rebranded as the "hanging judge" thanks to Arthur Miller's *The Crucible*. According to local tour guides, Hawthorne added the *w* to his name to distance himself from his great-great-grandfather. However, there is no proof that the *Scarlet Letter* writer abhorred his familial connections to the 1692 witch-trial hysteria.

As far as the curses associated with Salem, Hawthorne seemed to be fascinated by them. For example, he's one of the first people to write about the Giles Corey hex. Hawthorne claimed that the apparition "of the wizard appears as a precursor to some great calamity impending over the community."

He was also inspired by the "God will give you blood to drink" curse supposedly uttered by Sarah Good and directed at the Reverend Nicholas Noyes. In his *House of the Seven Gables*, witch-trials victim Matthew Maule hexes his accuser, Colonel Pyncheon. In both the book and in real life, Pyncheon and Noyes respectively choked to death on their own blood.

While Hawthorne is responsible for perpetuating the lore associated with Salem's curses, did he believe in the Witch City's ghosts? Based on the themes he explored in his books, the iconic author may have, but he definitely had a healthy dose of skepticism.

Hawthorne's friend William Baker Pike worked with him at the Salem Custom House in the 1840s. Pike, a Swedenborgian spiritualist, strongly believed in the idea of communicating with the dead. However, the author initially had his doubts. "Hawthorne was a skeptic, but he treated Pike's belief with respect," wrote Margaret Moore in *The Salem World of Nathaniel Hawthorne*.

In fact, Hawthorne wrote about his skepticism in a letter to Pike dated July 24, 1851: "I should be very glad to believe that these rappers are, in any one instance, the spirits of the persons whom they profess themselves to be; but though I have talked with those who have had the freest communication, there has always been something that makes me doubt."

While Hawthorne was initially a skeptic, he started to explore the possibility of the existence of spirits in his fiction. *The House of the Seven Gables* hinted at the supernatural with one character, Alice Pyncheon, being driven mad by a spell and dying from shame. Her spirit haunted the gabled house. Also, the building's original owner, Matthew Maule, makes a postmortem return to his ancestral dwelling in the novel.

Hawthorne's skeptical tune changed later in his life. In a story written in hindsight and published posthumously, the author claimed that he had a close encounter with a haunting while hanging out at the Boston Athenaeum, a members-only research facility considered to be the nation's oldest library, founded in 1807. It was a private gentleman's club, hosting luminaries such as Henry Wadsworth Longfellow, Henry David Thoreau, and, of course, Hawthorne, who read books and shared ideas.

Yes, it was a gentleman's club—no, not that kind of gentleman's club.

According to his published account called "The Ghost of Doctor Harris," the famed writer in residence was eating breakfast one morning at the library's former Pearl Street location when he noticed a familiar face reading the *Boston Post*. It was Dr. Thaddeus Mason Harris, a well-known Unitarian clergyman from Dorchester, sitting in his usual chair in front of the library's second-floor fireplace. Hawthorne didn't bother the old patriarch. However, he was shocked to learn later that day that the Athenaeum regular had passed away.

Hawthorne returned to the Athenaeum the following day and noticed, completely in shock, Harris sitting at his usual spot and reading the newspaper. Yep, Hawthorne spotted the deceased doctor, looking "gaseous and vapory," and he was completely dumbfounded.

According to the printed account, Hawthorne spotted Harris's ghost for six weeks, and he later told his editor that he wished he had confronted the apparition. He wanted to ask him, "So, what's it like to be dead?" or at least find out if the old man knew he had passed. In fact, Hawthorne joked with his editor about the Harris encounter, saying, "Perhaps he finally got to his obituary and realized he was dead."

For the record, several books on Salem's ghost lore, including Robert Ellis Cahill's *Ghostly Haunts*, claimed that Hawthorne's encounter with Harris was at the Salem Athenaeum. Not true. While the author frequented Salem's private library to learn about his familial ties to the 1692 witch-trials hysteria, his run-in with the old-man spirit was in Boston.

Currently located at 337 Essex Street, the Salem counterpart of the private library was moved around during Hawthorne's lifetime. After studying at Bowdoin College in Maine, Hawthorne returned to Salem in 1825. He frequented the 34 Front Street location between 1841 and 1857, as well as the second floor of Plummer Hall, which is now the Phillips Library owned by the Peabody Essex Museum.

Whether Hawthorne actually believed in ghosts or merely used paranormal manifestations as a metaphorical device is a moot point. He was an inspiration for future writers, including horror author H. P. Lovecraft, who called *The House of the Seven Gables* one of "New England's greatest contributions to weird literature."

It's believed that Lovecraft's short stories "The Shunned House" "
and "The Picture in the House" were inspired by *Seven Gables*.

After penning his famous fictional account of New England's
Puritanical past, Hawthorne left Salem for good in late 1850. The
notoriously melancholic author set up shop in the Berkshires and
wrote *The House of the Seven Gables*, arguably the most important
examination of Salem's mystique, in 1851. The following year, he
and his family moved to a Concord estate formerly occupied by
Amos Bronson Alcott and called it "The Wayside." While on tour
in Plymouth, New Hampshire, Hawthorne died in his sleep on
May 19, 1864, and was buried in an area known as "Author's Ridge"
in Concord's Sleepy Hollow Cemetery.

While he left his mark in various cities, Hawthorne will be
forever remembered as Salem's native son.

NATHANIEL HAWTHORNE'S HAUNT:
TURNER-INGERSOLL MANSION

When asked about the alleged hauntings at the Turner-Ingersoll
Mansion, tour guides with the House of the Seven Gables were
quick to dispel the rumors during my first visit in 2013. "Nope, hav-
en't heard of any ghosts," remarked one veteran tour guide walking
a large group up the now-famous secret staircase to what is believed
to be the structure's haunted attic. Another guide merely said that
the house "can get creepy at night."

Meanwhile, the eyes of the Victorian-era paintings dotting the
beloved inspiration for Nathaniel Hawthorne's Gothic masterpiece,
The House of the Seven Gables, eerily seemed like they were following
the group as the tour quietly shuffled from one room to the next.

No way. It's not haunted. Or is it?

Several books on ghost lore list the Turner-Ingersoll House, built in 1668, as one of Salem's most active. However, some of the information is based purely on conjecture. "Nathaniel Hawthorne, descendent of one of the witchcraft judges, was born in Salem in 1804 and always felt that the home of cousin Susan Ingersoll was haunted," wrote Dennis Hauck in *Haunted Places*. "He put his impressions on paper in the famous horror novel whose name the house now bears. The House of the Seven Gables is considered to be one of the eeriest in a town full of haunted houses."

Other stories suggest that Ingersoll, who inherited the house from her ship captain father after John Turner III lost the family fortune, has been spotted roaming the house's hallways. According to reports, she eerily peeks out of the windows when visitors are frolicking in the museum's beautifully manicured gardens. Yes, she's supposedly keeping watch over the droves of people touring her former home.

Another tale involves a ghost kid who plays in the Turner-Ingersoll House's attic. The sounds of disembodied footsteps and laughter have been heard in the top floor when no one, at least among the living, is up there. Oddly, the attic is where the Turner family's servants and indentured servants slept. Re-created sleeping quarters are visible when touring the house, and one room, located under one of the attic's gables, is armed with a child's rocking chair and sleeping mat. Perhaps this is where the boy specter plays.

Also, there's a blog post circulating online about a close encounter with what is believed to be the ghost of Hawthorne's son, Julian, peeking over a fence in the garden. "I decided to take a guided tour of the House of the Seven Gables property, also known as the Turner-Ingersoll Mansion located at 54 Turner Street," wrote Lisa from Long Island. "On that property now sits the birth home of American author Nathaniel Hawthorne, which was actually moved from Union Street onto Turner Street."

The woman shot a photo of what looked like a boy or, as others have suggested, a smudge on her camera lens or a wayward squirrel. The editor used an archival photo of Hawthorne's son to positively identify the so-called paranormal photo.

For the record, neither Hawthorne nor his son ever lived in the Turner House.

There is also lore associated with the secret staircase, built in 1908, which leads visitors to the attic, which is rumored to be haunted. According to several reports, people have witnessed the phantom of a man believed to be a slave trekking up and down the stairs. Some say that the Turner House, which was originally much smaller with only two and a half floors, was an end stop on the Underground Railroad. However, the hidden steps were built almost fifty years after slavery was abolished, so it's highly unlikely it's a residual haunting of a slave.

Philanthropist Caroline Emmerton founded the present-day museum and created the staircase with the help of architect Joseph Everett Chandler, known for his Colonial Revival aesthetic, in 1908. Yes, the stairs are creepy, and the journey to the attic can be a tad claustrophobic, but the hidden passageway is probably not active.

Then there is the final stop on the tour, Hawthorne's birthplace, which was moved from Union Street to its present-day location across from the Turner House in 1958. This red Georgian-style structure is definitely more eerie than its supposedly haunted neighbor. According to Lynda Lee Macken's *Haunted Salem & Beyond*, a seamstress ghost inhabits the house. "Her spirit has been seen sewing and walking in the house," Macken claimed.

Based purely on lore, the House of the Seven Gables campus is home to five ghosts—and a handful of living tour guides who vehemently deny their existence.

But is it really haunted?

Paranormal investigators haven't yet had access to either the Turner House or Hawthorne's birthplace. Only anecdotal evidence exists. However, Adam Berry from *Kindred Spirits* told me to rely on one's intuition when checking out spots with alleged paranormal activity. "As investigators, we try not to go on feelings, because you can't prove feelings," Berry said. "But you can't ignore your biggest organ, which is your skin, and the goose bumps that you get and feeling like you're being watched."

Heeding Berry's advice, I signed up to give tours at the House of the Seven Gables in October 2017 so I could check out the location for myself. After giving dozens of tours during the museum's busy season, I didn't have a paranormal experience in the actual Turner-Ingersoll Mansion. Oddly, it was during a tour led by a fellow guide in April 2018 that I had a haunted encounter in the museum's attic. I felt as if someone, or something, was tugging on my shirt as if it was trying to get my attention. Was it a ghost kid? Yes, I'm sure of it.

While I'm not convinced that the main house is actually haunted except for the attic, I can say without hesitation that the other historical structures on campus—including Hawthorne's birthplace, the Hooper-Hathaway House, and the Retire Beckett House—are paranormally active.

One day after giving tours, I was clocking out at the Hooper-Hathaway House and the door literally slammed in my face. I then heard a female voice say "stay" and noticed that my jacket was somehow stuck in the door handle. I had to ask a coworker to help me untangle my sleeve so I could leave the historic structure, built in 1682.

During a visit at the Retire Beckett House, which is home to the gift shop, I was looking for a copy of my book, *Ghosts of Salem*, for a guest on my tour. After looking through the stacks, I watched in awe as my book literally flew off the shelf and landed on the floor in front of me.

Haunted? Um, yes.

Thomas Barnard

Did Thomas Barnard, the assistant minister to the Reverend Francis Dane in Andover during the witch trials of 1692, get a bum rap? Gregg Pascoe, the caretaker of the Parson Barnard House in present-day North Andover, believes he did.

"For many years people unfairly judged him because they assumed he was a driving factor during the Salem witch trials, particularly in the episode that happened here where over fifty people were accused," Pascoe told me during a tour of the historic property. "But that's not the case."

Dane, on the other hand, was involved in a witch trial thirty years prior, where he testified against spectral evidence.

While the seventy-six-year-old Dane was vehemently opposed to the trials that were unfolding in nearby Salem Village, the young Barnard was fresh out of Harvard and wanted to make a name for himself at the parsonage. Historians believed that Reverend Barnard invited two of the afflicted girls—Mary Walcott and Ann Putnam Jr.—to attend the prayer meetings that included "touch tests" involving Andover's upper crust.

Pascoe said Barnard delivered the opening prayer at the infamous church service in September 1692 when all hell broke loose. "The afflicted girls started touching people, and they ended up arresting seventeen people for witchcraft on the spot," Pascoe said. "Because he started the service, people assumed that Barnard sanctioned the whole process and was in on bringing in the girls. He wasn't."

With the touch test, the afflicted would put their hands on the innocent people of Andover, and if they stopped having a fit, that townsperson was a witch. Oddly, several members of Reverend Dane's family were accused using this so-called test, including his two daughters and five of his grandchildren.

People assumed that Barnard was feuding with Dane and then orchestrated the touch test surprise. "In reality, Barnard wasn't an instigator during the church service," Pascoe explained. "He was just as surprised as everybody else."

Pascoe said the afflicted girls were like rock stars and the locals, including the extremely ill Timothy Swan, started a whole second wave of accusations. Because Barnard went to Harvard, people automatically assumed that he and the Reverend Cotton Mather were somehow in cahoots. "I'm sure they knew each other, but I don't think they were buddies at Harvard," Pascoe said.

Were Barnard and Dane feuding reverends? It's possible. When Andover hired Barnard in 1682, they stopped paying Dane and gave the new minister in town a full salary. After Dane protested to officials in Boston, the church was required to split Barnard's pay with Dane. Of course, the town complied with the order. However, they divided the money unevenly. "They both were unhappy," Pascoe told me. "Barnard felt like he should get a full salary and so did Dane."

When Pascoe gave tours at the Parson Barnard House, he initially portrayed Barnard as a bad guy. "I started to incorporate the information that he was somehow a conspirator," the caretaker told me. "Every time I did that, the fire alarms in the house would mysteriously go off."

Pascoe took the alarms as a sign from beyond. "At that point, I started to question the information about Barnard. I felt like it wasn't correct. I started to incorporate the correct history on my tours and the fire alarms stopped going off. I believe it's him trying to correct me."

The elderly Dane was the driving force behind putting a stop to the trials in Andover. In fact, he wrote a petition in October 1692 addressing what he believed to be forced confessions of guilt made by the victims during the touch test frenzy. Fifty people were accused of witchcraft in Andover during the witch trials, and it's estimated that 80 percent of the town's residents had been affected in some way by the hysteria.

Three innocents—including Martha Carrier, Mary Parker, and Samuel Wardwell—were executed before Reverend Dane was able to intercede.

THOMAS BARNARD'S HAUNT: PARSON BARNARD HOUSE

Built in 1715, the Parson Barnard House in North Andover was a later-in-life homestead for the reverend who was wrongly blamed as an instigator during the Salem witch trials. According to the historic property's caretaker, Gregg Pascoe, the Reverend Thomas Barnard died a few years after the house was built.

His previous home, the town's parsonage in Andover, mysteriously caught on fire and burned to the ground. "He lived here for three years," Pascoe told me as we explored the three-hundred-year-old property. "They started work on it in 1714, and it was completed one year later."

Pascoe isn't exactly sure how the reverend passed. "I heard that he had an illness, but I've also read that he had a stroke," the caretaker told me. Pascoe doesn't know the details of Barnard's death. But, he's convinced the home's first owner is lingering there in the afterlife.

When Pascoe first moved into the house in 2012, he heard a disembodied voice utter his name in the attic. "I had just moved in and I was giving family members a tour of the house," he recalled. "When I walked up the stairs, I heard my name."

The caretaker said the paranormal activity continued for years. Walking through the structure was like stepping back in time. Each step had a story.

During my tour with Pascoe, I noticed that there was dried sage hanging throughout the structure, which added to its already-eerie aesthetic. "Back in their day, sage was an herb that they used for flavoring food and medicinal purposes. They even dyed clothing with some herbs," Pascoe said. "It wasn't unusual for dried sage to be hanging around the house."

When I asked Pascoe if colonists used sage to ward off spirits back in the 1700s, he shrugged. "I don't think it was used to cleanse homes in that era," he said. "At the same time, everybody believed in witchcraft back then. Did they know it could be used for cleansing? Probably. It could have been a folksy wisdom that they knew about."

In addition to Pascoe's firsthand experiences in the attic and the fire alarm sounding off when he incorrectly told Barnard's story, the caretaker said the ghostly activity intensified when he invited paranormal investigators and mediums to check out the property.

He watched in awe when he saw a penny being slung by a dis-embodied spirit in the Parson Barnard House. "There were tons of coins in this house," Pascoe told me. "I figured the former caretaker left them." He joked that he collected the loose change for beer money, but he missed a few.

Pascoe said he was shocked when the resident ghosts figured out how to manipulate the coins. "Pennies were flying through the air," he told me.

The property also showcases an original seventeenth-century book called *Concordance* owned by the reverend. "One medium asked me if she could touch it," Pascoe said. "She then heard a male voice say 'Don't touch my book' and she quickly pulled away."

In 2017 I recommended the Parson Barnard House to the producers of the television show *Haunted Towns*. One of the investigators from the Tennessee Wraith Chasers, Steven "Doogie" McDougal, was terrorized in the structure's attic. While sitting in a chair, his leg was tugged. Oddly, the word "yank" appeared on the Ovilus when he was sitting in isolation.

Tim Weisberg, one of the producers from the TV show, set up an investigation after watching Doogie appear to be physically accosted by an unseen force. "I found out about the Parson Barnard House through working on *Haunted Towns*," Weisberg told Wicked Local. "When I saw how the Salem episode turned out, and the experiences the cast had at the Parson Barnard House, I knew I wanted to check it out."

Pascoe said Weisberg's investigation was intense. "He asked the ghost to move this penny," he said, showing me the coin that mysteriously was thrown at an investigator. Weisberg set up his flashlight on the dresser as he asked the entity to move the penny. The caretaker said the flashlight moved instead.

"The penny didn't move, but the spirit energy moved the flashlight," Pascoe added.

WICKED EXPERT: PETER MUISE

"Salem has learned its lesson and is probably the least likely place to have a witch hunt in the modern world."
—Peter Muise, *New England Folklore*

Is Salem cursed? For Peter Muise, author of *Legends and Lore of the North Shore* and founder of the blog *New England Folklore*, it's not an open-and-shut case.

"There's something weirdly ambiguous about a witch's curse," he told me. "Most often the curses are called down on the people who have harmed the witch and are a form of posthumous justice. The alleged witch is usually innocent of the crimes

Author Peter Muise is the founder of the *New England Folklore* blog.
PHOTO BY SAM BALTRUSIS

they are accused of, which is why the curse is effective after their death. But if the witch is really innocent of witchcraft, how are they capable of casting a curse? It's unclear."

As New England's folklore expert, Muise believes that stories involving witchcraft mysteriously tap into our subconscious fears. "It could be that you're afraid of the evil witch who is in league with Satan," he said, "or you're afraid of the self-righteous witch hunters or you're afraid of the witch's curse. Witchcraft stories are just uncanny."

When it comes to curses in Salem, the bulk of the bad blood can be traced back to 1692. There are two famous legends linked to the witch-trials era that continue to haunt the city.

First, there are the words supposedly uttered by Giles Corey, who was pressed to death over a two-day period. "Corey was an elderly farmer accused of witchcraft during the trials, but he refused to answer any questions when interrogated," Muise explained. "He just remained silent. Salem's sheriff was determined to make him talk. He staked Corey to the ground in a field and piled rocks on top of his body in an effort to make him speak."

Before taking his last breath, he told the sadistic sheriff George Corwin, "I curse you and Salem." According to lore, Corey's spirit appears when tragedy is about to strike. In fact, several people claimed that the "old wizard," words used by author Nathaniel Hawthorne, appeared to several locals right before the great Salem fire of 1914.

"Local tradition claims Corey's only words before being crushed to death were 'more weight,' but also claims that he cursed anyone who served as Salem's sheriff," Muise said. Corwin, who mysteriously died of a heart attack in 1696, was the first of several sheriffs who died of heart-related ailments. "The curse supposedly lasted until the Essex County sheriff's office was finally moved to Middleton in the late twentieth century," Muise added.

Then there is the famous hex unleashed by Sarah Good, a pipe-smoking vagabond who was executed as a witch on July 19, 1692. The object of her scorn? The Reverend Nicholas Noyes. He was the assistant minister at First Church and lived on Washington Street just opposite accused Bridget Bishop's house. Noyes was actively involved in the prosecution of many of the alleged witches and is known for calling the eight innocent victims dangling in the Gallows Hill area "firebrands of hell."

According to accounts, Reverend Noyes demanded a confession from Good. She shot back and called the reverend a liar. "I am no more a witch than you are a wizard," she said. "And if you take away my life, God will give you blood to drink."

Good had no way of knowing at the time that her words would come true. "Reverend Noyes died several years later from a brain hemorrhage," Muise explained. "As he expired blood gushed from his mouth, and his family remembered the curse that Sarah Good had uttered."

Nathaniel Hawthorne alluded to Good's curse in his classic *The House of the Seven Gables*. In the book, witch-trial character Matthew Maule curses his accuser, Colonel Pyncheon. Although historical record suggested that Good spewed her last words at Noyes, Hawthorne believed the venom was directed at his great-great-grandfather, Judge John Hathorne.

While the curses associated with the Salem witch trials have passed down through generations as cautionary tales, Muise isn't convinced that the Witch City is actually hexed.

"Those are very specific curses, and personally, I don't think the entire city of Salem is cursed," he said. "Salem has done a good job acknowledging what happened in 1692. The city celebrates witches in a variety of ways, whether it's memorializing the innocents who were executed or welcoming modern Wiccans."

Muise strongly believes that Salem has a history of remembering the mistakes from its witch-hunting past. "In 1811 a young woman from Boston moved to Salem and began to have fits," he explained. "She claimed the fits were being caused by a witch, but Salem's leaders weren't buying her story. They told her she could either leave town or go to the workhouse. She fled to Maine. And in 1878 a woman accused a local Christian Science practitioner of bewitching her. The trial was heard in the Salem courthouse, and the presiding judge dismissed it. He didn't want another witch trial in Salem."

When it comes to the history of cursed cities in the region, Muise said the Witch City isn't alone. The author rattled off a list of tall-tale curses unleashed by alleged witches throughout New England. "A village in North Pepperell, Massachusetts, was supposedly cursed by a Quaker woman who the villagers accused of witchcraft. The village's river dried up, its children sickened and died, and eventually the entire settlement was abandoned," he said. "In Bucksport, Maine, a boot mark on the grave of Colonel Jonathan Buck is explained as being caused by a dying witch's curse, while folklore from Plymouth mentions a witch named Aunt Rachel, who cursed the men who killed her family with her dying breath."

However, not everyone agrees with Muise's assessment that there is no lingering negativity associated with the hysteria unleashed by the city's Puritan forefathers. Locals who have experienced some of the bad mojo firsthand feel that Salem has endured more than three hundred years of tortuous penance.

"If you look at Salem's history, it has an amazing tradition of bad karma," explained Tim Maguire, historian and owner of the Salem Night Tour. "The wealthy of Salem made their blood money as privateers during the Revolution. Our history is tarnished with bad events and bad karma. I feel like the energy here is more negative than it is in other places. The witches in Salem call it the spirit of place."

If what goes around does come around, Muise believes Salem has somehow reversed the curse.

"Salem has learned its lesson and is probably the least likely place to have a witch hunt in the modern world," he concluded. "Terrible things happened there in the past, but I don't think there is a curse on the city."

Cursed? Perhaps. Haunted? Absolutely.

Maguire, in comparison to Muise, has a more *X-Files*-style explanation as to why some consider Salem to be cursed land. "There's an energy here that's different. I feel it a lot stronger in Salem than, say, Boston," Maguire said. "A lot of places like Gettysburg and the Bermuda Triangle, there tends to be electrical issues. Salem has an electrical fault under the city. People who visit here notice that their cell phones drain fast. There are electrical oddities that were noticed by the Native Americans in 1618. They considered it a spiritual place and thought it was odd that Europeans wanted to stay in Salem."

Maguire said these electrical anomalies explain why Salem is supposedly a hotbed for the paranormal. "The Native Americans talked about seeing things here . . . or feeling a presence here," he continued. "When I'm doing a paranormal investigation in Salem, I have to let people know that when they put their meter on the ground, they're going to pick up stuff because Salem has an electrical issue."

As far as paranormal activity, the real-life horror of 1692 possibly created what experts call an "aura of disaster," or an environment that triggers ghostly happenings. But what came first . . . did spirits exist in pre-Puritan Salem?

The Naumkeag tribe, which was basically annihilated by a smallpox outbreak, believed the land was cursed with negative spirit energy. Spectral evidence, a form of testimony based on dreams and visions, was used by the so-called afflicted girls and up to fifty locals, which resulted in more than 150 arrests, 54 confessions, 28 convictions, 19 hangings, 5 deaths due to the horrific conditions of the jails, and the crushing-by-stone death of Giles Corey over a two-day period.

Were the ghosts of Salem to blame? Approaching the witch-trials hysteria with a paranormal lens, it's possible that poltergeists and other entities played a role in what became a cautionary tale of the dangers of religious extremism and the importance of due process. Based on Maguire's perspective, Salem was cursed long before 1692.

The Parson Barnard House in North Andover was featured on Destination America's *Haunted Towns*. PHOTO COURTESY OF FRANK C. GRACE

WICKED TAILS: SALEM'S GHOST CATS

"The light was off, and I was in the bathroom.
I swear to God a cat rubbed up against me."
—Brandon O'Shea, Bunghole Liquors

Spirits with Salem's spirits? During the Prohibition era, Bunghole Liquors on Derby Street had a past life as a funeral home. However, what was happening downstairs was enough to the raise the dead. Locals would gather next to the parlor's embalming equipment, down some illegal booze, and hang out in a spot that housed the city's recently deceased.

"Liquor flowed freely in the funeral parlor basement, the same place where the bodies were embalmed," confirmed the Bunghole's website. "One of the owner's drinking buddies

Bunghole Liquors has a past life as a funeral home and is reportedly haunted by ghost cats. PHOTO BY SAM BALTRUSIS

is rumored to have told him, 'If Prohibition is ever lifted, you should turn this place into a liquor store.' So in 1933, he did just that. One of the original owner's relatives (interestingly, a Polish priest who was being ordained) suggested The Bunghole as an official name."

The liquor store's quirky moniker was a slang term used by the locals to refer to the group's secret drinking spot. For the record, a "bunghole" is the hole in a cask or barrel. It's a fitting nickname since the liquor store is literally across the street from the city's once-thriving Derby Wharf.

Apparently, the original owner would smuggle in the illegal spirits using an underground tunnel connecting the structure to the wharf. Most of the booze was hidden in barrels.

"They had the second liquor license to be issued in the city after Prohibition," wrote Christopher Dowgin in *Salem Secret Underground*. "So the corpses moved out, the embalming tubes were buried in the walls and the tunnels were closed."

According to the Bunghole's website, the ghosts from its funeral parlor past still linger in the basement: "If you crept downstairs and tore down a few walls today, you'd notice the embalming tubes and no doubt a few empty flasks, left behind from the ancestors of The Bunghole, who occasionally haunt their old, secret hangout."

Brandon O'Shea, the assistant manager at Bunghole Liquors, confirmed the rumors with *Wicked Salem*. "This place is definitely haunted," he said. "I came here, and I heard it was haunted, but I never believed it."

O'Shea said a few encounters with the paranormal at the liquor store has challenged his lifelong skepticism. "The light was off, and I was in the bathroom," he recalled. "I swear to God a cat rubbed up against me. I'm not a believer in that sort of thing, but I ran out and asked [a coworker] if there was a cat or dog in the building. He said, 'No.' There was nothing there. All I know is that something touched my leg."

In addition to the ghost cat, the former skeptic said a full-bodied apparition of a woman mysteriously walked around the shop on a recent New Year's Eve. "We just had a big rush," O'Shea recalled. "My coworker saw this woman walk behind the wine rack and go out back. It's two hours later, and my other coworker bumped into a woman, but there was no one there."

O'Shea said he stays away from the basement area that formerly housed Bunghole Liquor's illegal speakeasy. "One of the cameras downstairs picked up white lights," he said. "When you're working alone, you always see weird things here. I'm telling you, I'm the last person ever to believe in this stuff. But something is here."

So what rubbed up against O'Shea's leg? According to Susanne Saville's *Hidden History of Salem*, a gaggle of ghost cats prowl the city at night. "For the Halloween capital of the world, Salem's ghost population is surprisingly small. And furry," she mused, alluding to the feline spirit allegedly haunting the Stephen Daniels House inn.

There's also an odd incident at the Witch House from 1897 involving photographer Walter Sprange. "In the view presented one of the most woe-begotten, ill-shaped cats," Sprange wrote, saying a feline spirit was peering out of the open casement. "In another view taken it appears in the doorway." Apparently, Sprange captured a spectral kitty peeking out of the rear of the Witch House. However, he only mentioned them in his notes and never published the photos.

Both Nathaniel Hawthorne and witch-trials victim Giles Corey loved the four-legged felines. In the early nineteenth century, a legendary cat called Pompey lived in Salem. She crossed the Atlantic in the Americas' first yacht, *Cleopatra's Barge*, owned by wealthy Salemite Benjamin Crowninshield. "We found a yellow cat lying on the bed," reported one of the barge's visitors. "The captain said she came on board on her own accord, and had chosen her position. He intended to take her with him for good luck." Pompey passed in 1817. However, it's possible that her spirit is wandering the streets of Salem and somehow made a pit stop at the Bunghole. Yes, it seems that cats do indeed have nine lives.

Looking for a room with a "boo," or would a "meow" suffice? Patrons at the historic Stephen Daniels House swear a phantom feline roams the inn and creeps in and out of rooms. Catherine "Kay" Gill purchased the property in the early '60s and was the Stephen Daniels House owner and innkeeper for over fifty years. Gill, a local legend, passed in 2018. Apparently, she didn't suffer from cat-ghost fever.

"In 1953, ten years before she bought the inn, she painted a portrait of a gray tabby," wrote Cheri Revai in *Haunted Massachusetts*. "When she moved in, she hung the portrait in the Rose Room—the same room guests tell her is haunted by a gray-and-black striped cat that looks just like the one in the painting."

The oldest bed-and-breakfast in Salem was built in 1667 by Captain Stephen Daniels and served as the private residence of his descendants for over three decades. Daniels's great-grandson, Samuel Silsbee, extended the house in 1756. Before becoming an overnight haunt, it was converted into a private two-family residence for a few years. It remained vacant until 1945, when the Haller family transformed the structure into a restaurant and inn. Gill purchased the historic building in 1963.

"Kay herself has never heard so much as a purr," continued Revai. "But her patrons assure her that she does, indeed, have a ghost or two, and that's OK with them."

One of the more popular spirits spotted at the Stephen Daniels House is a full-bodied apparition of a man who bears a striking resemblance to a man featured in a painting hanging in the dining room of the classic Colonial structure. Gill told Revai that "a guest sleeping in the great room had a visit from a man in a shiny black suit and top hat who, from the description, looked remarkably like Stephen Daniels." According to Gill's description, the male apparition appears to be an intelligent haunting and is known to say "Welcome to the house" to overnight visitors.

Based on previous interviews with paranormal experts, it's common for a building's original owner to stick around a few centuries after their death.

"Spirits are attracted to the places they lived in," opined the late Jim McCabe, who was a noted ghost-lore expert in Boston. "I think what attracts ghosts up here is that you don't tear down the buildings."

Adam Berry from *Kindred Spirits* echoed McCabe's belief. "My theory is that when one person works so hard to build an empire, whether it's a city, a business, or an estate, they can still be around trying to check on what's going on and how those who are still there are running the place," Berry said. "I absolutely believe that New England has tons of spirits because it was the center of everything. People were building empires, and the more energy that surrounds that kind of situation, the more likely there will be spirits lingering about."

Of course, it could merely be the Stephen Daniels House's sentinel spirit. "The motif of the haunted house is a deep-rooted one, perhaps having its origin in the ancient belief that each place, including dwellings, had its own 'genuis loci,' which in Roman mythology meant the protective deity/spirit of a location, but which could be the place's distinctive spirit," wrote Brian Haughton in *Lore of the Ghost*.

The third spirit is an alleged residual haunting of a woman who replays her tragic fall down the stairs. "At least one guest to the inn has seen the woman descend one of the staircases inside the house," wrote Mark Jasper in *Haunted Inns of New England*. "It should be noted that the ghost appears none too nimble or perhaps there have been renovations since the first time she set foot in the Daniels house . . . for the ghost has been known to fall down the stairs as she attempts to descend them."

Of course, the ghost cat appears to be the most common apparition spotted in the Colonial-era building. "No one knows where the cat comes in, although for a house in Salem to exist without a cat would have to be some sort of minor miracle," wrote Saville in *Hidden History of Salem*. "In any case, guests have repeatedly commented on the tabby, only to be told the inn has no cats."

Revai joked that the return visitors to the inn say the cat ghost is part of the Stephen Daniels House's charm. "Return customers even remember to leave a bowl of milk out at night, hopeful that they'll once again encounter their furry friend."

WICKED EXCURSION: USS *SALEM*

"I could see them through the curtain and
two of the girls had scratches all up and down
their legs . . . and they were bleeding."
—Kim Mello, USS *Salem* volunteer

The other haunted Salem, the *Sea Witch*, summoned me like a Greek siren seducing sailors with beautiful music only to devour them later with a maenadic ferocity. She was ruthless.

I see dead people. And in one recent nightmare that turned my life upside down, I also channel them. The entity attached itself to me a few days after I fled a high-profile management position aboard the USS *Salem* in nearby Quincy, Massachusetts.

It happened at a place that I thought was safe. The event was called the Haunting at Witch Hill, and I was asked to tell "spooky stories" wearing Victorian-era garb at the historic Peirce Farm in Topsfield, Massachusetts. I decided to retell the so-called crime of the century that riveted Salem back in 1830 and involved a black sheep family member of one of the structure's former owners.

It happened the night before Halloween 2016. My attachment was a murderer. His name? Richard Crowninshield. He savagely bludgeoned Captain Joseph White, an eighty-two-year-old shipmaster and trader, who was whacked over the head with a twenty-two-inch piece of refurbished hickory, also known as an "Indian club," and stabbed thirteen times near his heart.

I had no idea that my fractured fairy tale life was about to turn into a nightmare.

The reason I had such a low vibration? I was beat down spiritually, emotionally, and physically after trying the keep the

The USS *Salem* is home to a haunted attraction called Ghost Ship Harbor in October. Photo courtesy of Frank C. Grace

ghosts in check on a new monthlong haunted attraction called Ghost Ship Harbor held on the *Sea Witch*. We were haunting the haunted on the USS *Salem*. But truthfully the ghosts were haunting—and hunting—my team. It was too much for even the best empaths and psychics to endure. By the end of the 2016 Halloween season, they were dropping like flies.

Because of my previous experience running ghost tours in Boston and Salem, I was asked to manage the "VIP paranormal experience" on the Ghost Ship Harbor attraction, which operated from September through Halloween in 2016. I managed a crew of experienced investigators and newbie tour guides. This was the first time the USS *Salem* had a "haunted house" coupled with a paranormal investigation happening at the same time. Our patrons loved how we combined a haunted attraction on an actual haunted vessel. However, the USS *Salem*'s ghosts apparently didn't like it so much.

My first visit to the USS *Salem* was in early September 2016 with "hauntrepreneur" Jason Egan, owner of Fright Dome in Las Vegas. He produced the haunted house aspect of Ghost Ship Harbor. I toured the vessel on my own, letting the ghosts guide me.

I was immediately called to the third mess hall area near the stern of the heavy cruiser. I walked to the berthing area beneath the mess hall and encountered a child spirit that seemed to be around six. I literally saw the outline of a kid hiding in the corner when I entered the berthing area. I called out to him and he disappeared.

Unfazed by this encounter because of my history as an empath, I tried to go beneath the berthing area to what was known as the "butter room." This is where the bodies were kept during the Ionian earthquake in 1953. In turns out the ghosts on the USS *Salem* are tied to a horrific tragedy that happened in Greece, when the vessel served as a triage unit for victims of the earthquake. The hatch to the morgue area was bolted shut,

The third USS *Salem* (CA-139) is one of three Des Moines–class heavy cruisers completed for the United States Navy shortly after World War II. PHOTO COURTESY OF FRANK C. GRACE

so I quickly headed to the top deck. Before going upstairs, I noticed the chains on the stairs leading up to the top deck were inexplicably moving.

The idea of a scared child spirit haunting the USS *Salem* initially interested me more than it scared me. I accepted the job with Egan and Ghost Ship Harbor and quickly assembled a crew to work with me during the Halloween season. I had no idea what I was about to sign up for as the manager of Ghost Ship Harbor's paranormal experience on the USS *Salem*. The little boy spirit was just the tip of the ghostly iceberg that eventually became the scariest month of my life.

I spent the next few weeks interviewing people on board. According to one man working on the vessel who was originally from Greece, a female spirit spoke in his native language. She said, "είναι επιτέλους εδώ" or "eínai epitélous edó." The English translation of the disembodied woman's haunting words: "He is finally here."

I wrote a story for *DigBoston* and shot a segment for a local TV show. I heard all sorts of stories about paranormal encounters on the vessel, including a group of teen girls mysteriously getting scratched until they bled by an unseen entity.

Here's the initial story that ran in *DigBoston*:

The *Sea Witch* smells like death. "It's the paint," joked one of the volunteers who greeted me as I clumsily stumbled on board the historic USS *Salem* in Quincy. "There were hundreds of dead bodies on here during the earthquake in Greece in 1953 and many of them died from burns . . . so that could explain the peculiar smell as well."

One of the first things I was told when I reported for duty as the manager of the VIP paranormal experience on Ghost Ship

Harbor, a new haunted attraction slotted for the USS *Salem* this Halloween season, was not to piss off the ghosts.

Launched on March 25, 1947, in Fore River Shipyard in Quincy and nicknamed the *Sea Witch* by her crew thanks to a three-month stint in the Witch City, the USS *Salem* never saw combat but was certainly a harbinger of death. In fact, the area beneath her mess hall became a makeshift morgue during the previously mentioned earthquake off the coast of Greece in 1953 and it's estimated that at least 200 dead bodies were kept on the vessel. According to additional reports, at least one dozen babies were born on the ship during the 1950s.

The USS *Salem* is a heavy-metal celebrity of sorts. She made a cameo in the action-packed thriller from Disney called *The Finest Hours* starring Casey Affleck and Chris Pine. The vessel was also featured in a film called the *Pursuit of the Graf Spee* in 1956. And, of course, the haunted vessel was featured on *Ghost Hunters* a few years ago.

It should be no surprise but it's the ghost ship's alleged paranormal activity that generates the most regional buzz.

The USS *Salem*'s volunteers, a motley crew of former military veterans and lovers of the Des Moines–class heavy cruiser, spewed off a laundry list of resident ghosts including the "burning man," who also smells like death and reportedly hides in the berthing area beneath the third mess hall where the bodies were kept during the Ionian earthquake, a ghost girl who speaks Greek, a salty sea captain, a growling dog, a cook who likes to keep the kitchen in order and a man named John who reportedly gives tours of the USS *Salem* in the afterlife.

There's also an angry sentinel spirit known to get aggressive if you disrespect the *Sea Witch*.

Kim Mello, a long-time volunteer on the ship and former manager of the USS *Salem's* haunted house, told me about a group of teen-girl haunters who were banging on the freezers near the wardroom pantry. "I told them to stop disrespecting the spirits but they wouldn't listen," she said, describing the former horror-themed room full of "living dolls," a scene that caused a ruckus several seasons ago because one of the dolls naively said "turn me on" to visitors. "I could see them through the curtain and two of the girls had scratches all up and down their legs . . . and they were bleeding. I know they didn't do it to themselves because I was watching the whole thing as it happened."

Mello said the mysterious scratches were mere "love marks" compared to the nightmare her team of volunteer haunters endured when they were told to move the haunted house off of the boat. In 2013, access to the vessel was shut down because the MBTA deemed the wharf was unstable. In addition to hosting paranormal investigation teams and overnight visits for Boy Scout groups, the pocket battleship had a 20-year run as the U.S. Naval Shipbuilding Museum in Quincy and served as a symbol of the city's shipbuilding history during the 1940s.

"It was a nightmare," Mello said, referring to the volunteer group's attempt to resurrect the vessel's haunted attraction. "We had a circus freak show theme and we had a tough time keeping the tents up during the season. Plus, it was freezing."

Jason Egan, the hauntrepreneur behind Fright Dome in Las Vegas and mastermind behind the new attraction aboard the USS *Salem*, had an equally rough ride in his search for the ideal location to produce a Boston-area attraction. Egan and local marketing guru Matt DiRoberto were swatted down twice when they tried to unleash their initial vision called Fright Island on Georges Island and then Castle Island in South Boston.

Egan's dream of creating his world-class haunt on a Boston Harbor island was ultimately crushed. However, he and DiRoberto approached the USS *Salem* and they were eager to create a haunted house on a notoriously haunted location. For the record, the boat was ranked No. 8 in my *13 Most Haunted in Massachusetts* book released last year.

"We kind of fell into this location. Originally we were gearing for an island but then we came across this ship. This thing is huge and it's actually haunted. I'm very excited to launch this haunted attraction in such a unique and iconic location," said Fright Dome owner Jason Egan. "Over the years, my team has created some of the top Halloween events in the world, from Las Vegas to Hong Kong. To launch in a new market like Boston and work in a location that is notoriously haunted is amazing."

Rachel Hoffman, an investigator with Paranormal Xpeditions and one of the handful of experts working with me on Ghost Ship Harbor, said her team uncovered a lot of activity in the hospital unit. "We heard a crying baby in the medical area," she said, adding that there are tables with stirrups indicating facilities for childbirth. In the so-called "butter room" or "meat locker where the bodies were kept while at sea was the thickest, most active area," Hoffman told me in an interview for my book *13 Most Haunted in Massachusetts*, adding that her team heard banging and that others reported being touched when no one else was on board.

The USS *Salem* also boasts a few misogynistic spirits who frequently retaliated when Hoffman's all-female crew investigated the ship. For the record, the vessel was decommissioned in 1959 and its alleged spirits reflect the sentiment prevalent during the World War II era. "The most active was the admiral's quarters where we got EVPs," she continued. "The men didn't like ladies on their ship. I think the ghosts of the men who served still reside with their old-school rules." Paranormal Xpeditions also picked up an electromagnetic voice phenomenon, or EVP, of what sounded like a pig on the top deck.

The USS *Salem*'s proverbial ghost cat was let out of the bag in October 2009 when Syfy's *Ghost Hunters* investigated the 718-foot cruiser.

In the anchor windlass room, Michael Condon told the Atlantic Paranormal Society (TAPS) team that "one of our volunteers, his name was John, used to work in this space, maintaining and cleaning it. One day he passed away and we noticed people saying they met this terrific tour guide named John," the vessel's executive director Condon said, adding that they didn't have any tour guides on the ship at that time. "He's very active in this spot and people actively see him and even talk to him."

Tom Ventosi, a volunteer with the USS *Salem*, said he saw a woman in white in the restricted medical area. "As I looked down the hall, you could see a woman taking a right. She was in white shorts, white shirt and had a white handbag. She just turned and walked. And when we went down there and looked where she went there was only a metal wall. We couldn't find her anywhere."

Condon mentioned that he's heard an EVP of a woman in the medical area, near the tables with stirrups, saying "get out, get out." However, Condon said the agitated spirit could be saying "get it out" which could be a reference to the multiple children born on the USS *Salem*.

The executive director also told TAPS that he spotted a shadow figure in the machine shop. The ship's archivist, John

Connors, said he's heard phantom footsteps above him when he's working. "It's always right above my head," Connors explained. "I go up on the main deck to see if there are any cars in the parking lot and there are no cars there, except my truck. I look around to see if anybody is onboard . . . nobody."

The *Ghost Hunters* crew did pick up footsteps immediately and claimed to have heard a woman's voice. Grant Wilson said he saw a shadowy black figure creep up the gangplank. They also picked up high levels of electromagnetic activity which could result in uneasy feelings of paranoia.

During the reveal, they picked up a low-grade EVP and other inexplicable bumps in the night. "What does it come down to? We have some bangs that we can't explain and we have some low, subtle voices," said Wilson, mentioning his close encounter with the shadow figure.

"I truly believe there is something going on here," Jason Hawes confirmed. "I would like to come back and investigate."

If *Ghost Hunters* does return, the USS *Salem* will be secured at a different location. It's slotted to move in November a few docks away from its current location in Quincy. Over the past year, the vessel was rumored to set sail for the Boston Harbor Shipyard and Marina next to the Nantucket Lightship in East Boston and then Fall River. However, management decided it's best to keep her close to home.

Don DeCristofaro, a paranormal investigator who spent many sleepless nights on the USS *Salem*, said he's glad the vessel is staying nearby. In his opinion, the vessel is a paranormal goldmine since the *Ghost Hunters* team visited in 2009. "Interestingly, the ship became much more active after TAPS left," he said. "Numerous people claim that TAPS opened several doors for spirits on the ship and didn't close them when they left."

DeCristofaro said *Ghost Hunters* focused on the ship's least active areas, the anchor windlass room. "My most intense experiences have been in the wardroom and the mess decks. We had an evening in the wardroom where several chairs were overturned. The night was the only time I can honestly say I was uncomfortable on the ship. I really felt like something bad was with us that night."

DeCristofaro said he "lost some time" during the investigation. "The psychic I was with that night said I was channeling," he emoted. "It was very strange and I was bleeding when it was over."

Will the ghosts of the USS *Salem* draw blood this Halloween season? As the manager of Ghost Ship Harbor's VIP paranormal experience, I'm trying my damndest to not piss off the vessel's ghosts. So far . . . no blood. Anchors aweigh.

Little did I know when writing the article for *DigBoston*, the ghosts would continue to attack my staff and it would escalate as the Halloween season progressed.

When construction crews from Las Vegas started creating the haunted house elements on Ghost Ship Harbor in late September, it was as if the spirits on board were scared that unfamiliar outsiders were ripping their home apart. The ghosts retreated to the bowels of the vessel, it seems, and hid there while the haunted house event was going on. However, that didn't last for long.

On October 3 I welcomed a crew of paranormal investigators and filmmakers, including Ron Kolek, Steve Parsons, and Anne Kerrigan, on board the USS *Salem* to interview me about the ghost lore associated with the vessel for Kolek's local TV show, *Ghost Chronicles*. We filmed in the "séance room," which was where my staff held a portion of the paranormal experience.

It was located in the bow of the vessel in the admiral's quarters area, which is also known as the state room. It's normally not an active part of the USS *Salem*, but it seemed as if the ghosts performed on command.

During the interview with Kolek, objects started to mysteriously fall off the walls. The mirror in the room started to sway, and we heard a loud female scream. Ron thought the postmortem pleas from beyond were from the haunted house part of the vessel. They weren't. Our interview was on a Monday, and the haunted house was closed for the week. The most terrifying part of the experience was the extreme temperature change in the room. For the record, there is no heating or cooling on the vessel. The room went from cool to extremely hot within a few minutes. There is no rational explanation . . . except for what locals call the "burning man."

The burning man is believed to be either a victim of the earthquake in Greece or died after an explosion that happened in the Brooklyn Navy Yard. The USS *Salem* also rescued victims from that fire and served as a hospital triage unit.

Casey Johnson Huff, who visited the paranormal experience with me on Ghost Ship Harbor, said she was haunted by the burning man for weeks. "I had nightmares after being on the USS *Salem*," she told me. "It was of a person with flesh burning off them. I had nightmares for two weeks straight."

From October 3 on, the paranormal activity on the vessel started to intensify. We had hundreds of people join us every weekend and the ghosts seemed to get progressively upset. People were getting scratched and pushed by unseen entities. We picked up an EVP of what sounded like "Tell them to get the f--k out of here." On the vessel, I had an extremely difficult time keeping actors in the makeshift "séance room." They were doing a theatrical channeling session. However, inexplicable things started to happen, and I literally went through four people within two weeks. All of the actors playing the psychic role were terrified and felt like the spirits didn't want them there.

My friend Kristene Gulla, an actual professional psychic known as the Queen of Cups, was working outside as a vendor for most of the event. Gulla initially signed on to do makeup, but we had to bring her into the séance room because none of the psychic performers would stay. The first night she was in the séance room, the door mysteriously closed and I heard a voice in my ear say, "Get Kristene out now."

I ran to her. She was frozen, as if someone hit the "pause" button. As soon as I walked into the space, a candle was slung across the room. In that part of the vessel, we also physically witnessed rocks and all sorts of things inexplicably move.

Later that evening we found a haunter, one of the new employees on the ship, in a catatonic state. It was as if he had seen a ghost. He was pulled out of a hatch area into an ambulance. His dark skin turned white. His last words before being carted off in the ambulance: "There is something evil on that ship."

It was that weekend that I had an encounter with what looked like a shadow figure running at me. It dispersed into little pieces when it got closer., the shards of darkness like black shooting stars. We had multiple reports of this phenomenon that we collectively nicknamed "paranormal darts." Most of us during that monthlong event had an experience with the ship's so-called darts.

We had five tour guides altogether, and they were all flipping out. I had one who said she was unable to move in the séance room, as if something was holding her down. When the Queen of Cups would ask the group a question, Bianca would feel a presence force her head to move forward, simulating a nod, as if she was a puppet. The tour guide came to me in tears on a regular basis.

At this point, my job was to protect my employees and the hundreds of visitors who came on board. I started referring to the event as "Ghost Ship Hell."

One night in mid-October, fog was seeping into the lower deck of the vessel. I then spotted the outline of what looked like a little ghost boy. Was it the same child spirit I bumped into in early September? He started to run and I followed him to the bowel of the ship. I became disoriented and couldn't find my way out until the wee hours of the night. I was literally trapped for hours on the USS *Salem*. It was as if I somehow lost track of time.

The following evening the USS *Salem* made national headlines when several local teens broke into the vessel and stole some items. They didn't take much except for a few radios. I wouldn't be surprised if they were scared off the extremely haunted *Sea Witch*.

On Friday, October 21, the last weekend right before Halloween, it started to rain. The haunted house portion of Ghost Ship Harbor was designed by a crew from Las Vegas, so it seriously was dangerous during a rainstorm. I strongly felt that the haunt should have been shut down because of safety issues. The rain started to pour, and we had hundreds of people in line for the paranormal experience.

Bianca, the tour guide who was pinned to her chair with her head forcibly moved back and forth like a puppet, was convinced that the spirit in the séance room was trying to control her. She was hysterically crying, begging me to finish her tours for the evening. I agreed to do it, but what happened next continues to haunt me.

One of our paranormal investigators, Rachel Hoffman, picked up the word "poltergeist" over and over on her Ovilus. I had the realization at that moment—the paranormal activity was more than just a residual haunting or a lost child spirit. It was a poltergeist or a hyped-up intelligent haunting.

The rain continued to pour, and I was walking a group of twenty guests through the haunt in water that came up to my ankles. My flashlight stopped working and then my glasses fell off. I panicked. I was literally unable to see as I guided a group of people through the labyrinthine haunted house. The animatronics within the haunt started to malfunction. I started to hyperventilate. That evening literally felt like the finale pool scene in the movie *Poltergeist* from 1982.

As I was desperately looking for a way out, one of the guests found my glasses. I was able to see how dangerous the situation was at that point. There was an exposed generator

Paranormal Xpedition's Rachel Hoffman has heard a crying baby in the medical area. The tables with stirrups were used as facilities for childbirth.
PHOTO COURTESY OF FRANK C. GRACE

which was used to power the entire haunted attraction, and I was standing next to it in a pool of water.

I had enough.

After the traumatic experience, I resigned with a two-day notice. However, the paranormal activity continued full throttle until the last night I was on the USS *Salem* that season. In hindsight, the entity known as the burning man exhibited poltergeist-like characteristics, and it seemed to be feeding off the fear of all of the people who came on the ship.

It was during this emotionally raw period after I left Ghost Ship Harbor that I somehow picked up an attachment, or a disembodied entity that attached itself to my energy field. I was both spiritually and mentally off-kilter. It felt like I was surrounded by a cloud of frustration. During this emotionally painful experience, I reached out to the paranormal community for help.

Nick Groff, a pop-culture investigator from Destination America's *Paranormal Lockdown*, talked about his experiences with negative spirit attachments in a previous interview. "Positive and negative energies really do exist, and they can have a major effect on you and your well-being," Groff told me. "If something is going to attach itself to me after leaving a negative location, it's difficult to get rid of that energy when you go home. Mentally, I try to stay strong and eventually it depreciates. It goes away."

The TV investigator continued: "Sometimes certain situations take longer than others, but I try to close the door when I leave a location. I just block it out. If you don't, it tends to feed on negativity, and it intensifies when you go home."

My friend Joni Mayhan talked to her shaman contact, Michael Robishaw. Thanks to his remote-viewing work, I was able to identify my attachment. "The entity attached to you is a male, around twenty-six years old when he was killed," the shaman told me. "He has anxiety issues and is not happy at all. He likes to be loud and very obnoxious. He comes from a wealthy family."

The good news? Robishaw was able to "bind and banish" the attachment he picked up in my energy field. The bad news was that I knew exactly what attached itself to me. During the event at Peirce Farm at Witch Hill on the night before Halloween, I accidentally channeled the disgruntled spirit of Richard Crown-inshield, the crime-for-hire murderer of Captain Joseph White at the Gardner-Pingree House in 1830. He came from a wealthy family and, by most accounts, was loud and obnoxious. The fact that Robishaw said he was "killed" raised an investigative red flag and confirmed my reading at Peirce Farm. Crowninshield told me during the channeling session that he didn't commit suicide in prison and that he may have been murdered in 1830.

Another freakish thing that I uncovered and didn't know at the time was that Crowninshield was twenty-six when he sup-posedly committed suicide in prison. Robishaw nailed it. Another oddity is that Jack Kenna, profiled in this book, encountered an entity he also believes to be the accused murderer. Apparently, Crowninshield gets around.

For the record, this wasn't my only trip to the attachment rodeo. I had my first experience with a negative entity while living in New York City. During the summer of 2000, I was walking from my job on Broadway to my apartment in the East Village and had a close encounter with something inexplicable that has haunted me for years.

It felt like the frigid hand of death grabbing my ankle.

I was casually walking through Washington Square Park, a trek I had made hundreds of times, and clearly remember feeling something touch my ankle. I looked down, thinking someone was pulling a practical joke or a homeless person was hiding in the flower bed and trying to get my attention. No one was there.

I kept walking, and then I felt it again. The second time was more profound, as the disembodied hand frantically held on, and I remember reaching down to physically knock off the death grip of someone who was definitely not there.

I didn't tell a soul. I thought it was something explainable. Then it happened again.

On a particularly warm winter day a few months later and right around the same spot, the corner of Washington Square Park East, I felt the mysterious hand again. This time, it wasn't letting go.

I didn't even think about the possibility of it being a ghost. At this point in my life, I was wearing what I call "paranormal blinders" and quickly tried to shrug off the incident.

In hindsight, I believe the spirit was desperately trying to tell me something. Or worse, it was trying to attach itself to me.

Mayhan, author of *Dark and Scary Things*, told me that it's possible that the ghost I encountered at Washington Square Park was preying on my sensitivity to the paranormal. "I've had a few really horrible attachments," explained Mayhan. "One of them was the subject of my book *Soul Collector*."

Mayhan said sensitives are like beacons of light to the spirit realm. "Since everybody senses them differently, it's always difficult to say if you had an attachment or not. One big sign though is a personality change or sudden depression. Dark moods and a feeling of just not wanting to live anymore are pretty common. They don't have to touch us to attach to us, but it probably doesn't hurt. They've penetrated our shield."

After the second encounter in Washington Square Park, my mood did change. In fact, I was overwhelmed by negativity. I mysteriously started having issues with anxiety and would drink alcohol to self-medicate. It was as if the grim reaper had pulled me into the abyss. I was drowning with negative emotions, and my life started to spiral out of control.

It felt like the attachment was feeding off of my energy.

"Investigators often flock to haunted venues, needlessly paying tremendous amounts of money to hunt for a ghost, while passing several dozen ghosts on their way to the door. Ghosts are everywhere," Mayhan continued. "You'll find them lurking in places where you find groups of people. Shopping malls and movie theaters are prime locations, as are restaurants, hospitals, and churches. Most of the time the ghosts are happy to remain there, but occasionally they find one human they feel is worth following."

In July 2017 I returned to the USS *Salem,* hoping to find some closure. As someone who has been sober from alcohol and in the recovery community for years, I've learned that it's best to confront my fears instead of drinking them away.

Spirit attachments can be human or nonhuman. Photo courtesy of Frank C. Grace

During the investigation, I had the sensation of an energy passing through my body for just a second and then quickly leave. It was a familiar tingling sensation. "Something just passed through me," I said out loud. There was a jolt of electricity, and then I felt drained.

"Ghosts will pull energy where they can find it," explained author Mayhan. "A typical sign that a ghost is using your energy is the sensation of vibration. When they pull energy from us, sometimes their vibrational rate is different from ours, giving us the feeling that we are vibrating from the inside out."

On the top deck of the *Sea Witch*, I looked up at a larger-than-usual new moon. My return to the USS *Salem* was about new beginnings.

At this point, I unexpectedly did something that has taken me years to completely understand. I decided to let go. The only true negative attachment I had was the self-constructed prison I created in my head.

"It's time to face your shadow self," whispered a voice in the darkness. The ghosts of my past—the entities on the USS *Salem*, Richard Crowninshield, Salem, and the ghosts of Washington Square Park—will no longer haunt me. I took a deep breath and slowly exhaled.

No more fear.

Conclusion

When I first jumped off of the vessel *Naumkeag* on the rocky coastline of the once off-limits Bakers Island in Salem, I started to hyperventilate. I could see in my mind's eye a young girl, probably around thirteen years old. She was wearing late nineteenth-century garb and, from what I picked up that particularly windy June morning in Salem Harbor, she was waiting for me.

While doing research for *Wicked Salem*, I signed up to lead weekend tours to the allegedly haunted island. After a nightmarish season in the Witch City during the Halloween of 2013 before writing my book *Ghosts of Salem*, I swore I would never go back to the North Shore haunt that turned inexplicably dark, and oddly evil, as the season progressed.

I'm back. Well, kinda sorta. The sixty-acre island is about five miles off the coast of Salem. While I did do some preliminary research on Bakers Island, I had no clue about its haunted past. As we inched toward the rocks, I intuitively knew that I was about to step on a paranormally active hot spot. The ghost girl was waiting . . . and so was a living man.

The lightkeeper, Bill, greeted our vessel as we quietly landed ashore. Wearing what looked like a Harley-Davidson T-shirt, Bill was standing on the rocks, holding a garbage bag, while Essex

Bakers Island remained in the hands of the Colonial government until 1660, when the General Court granted a request by the town of Salem to annex both Bakers and Misery Islands.

Heritage's chief executive officer, Annie, quickly hopped off onto the slippery shore. "No ghost stories," Annie told me a few minutes before landing. The salty waters of the harbor spit in my face as *Naumkeag*'s captain John maneuvered past Marblehead during my first trip to Salem's shutter island. I had asked Annie if she knew the story of the Screeching Woman of Lovis Cove. "Never heard of it," she said with a familiar New England nod that oddly reminded me of Katharine Hepburn. I sheepishly smiled back.

When I spotted the ghost girl on Bakers Island, I decided to keep it a secret. As far as I knew, there were no deaths at the lighthouse that had been closed to the general public for seventy years. Besides, I promised my boss no ghost stories. I couldn't help myself.

Lightkeeper Bill did write about what he later referred to as a "gremlin" on Bakers.

"When I got to the beach I was going to row out to the *Whaler* and take a look at the engine," he wrote online a few days before my first visit. "The oars were gone. Brenda and I remember placing them in the boat and I then jammed them in to make sure they stayed. Two life jackets and a pair of shoes were untouched but the oars were gone. I can only assume that someone stole them. Pretty lousy."

Stolen oars? It's possible. However, my intuition suggested something else, an elemental. Whatever it was, the spirit wanted to play.

The *Naumkeag* came carrying gifts, several pieces of wood needed to build a makeshift gift shop on the island. As I explored the island's lighthouse, I had one of my *That's So Raven* moments. I somehow psychically replayed what seemed to be a horrific maritime tragedy. However, the ghost girl on the island was letting me know that she was fine and that she has found postmortem serenity there even though she died tragically more than one century ago.

According to local legend, Bakers Island was named after a man who was mysteriously killed on the island by a falling tree. While there's no proof of the story told by the late historian Edward Rowe Snow, we do know of a man named Robert Baker who was fatally hit by a piece of lumber in 1640 in the shipyard off of Salem. The island was deeded to Salem in 1660 and rented out to John Turner in 1670. For the record, Turner was famous for building the House of the Seven Gables.

On April 8, 1796, President George Washington agreed to appropriate $6,000 for a lighthouse, and a beacon was first lit on

January 3, 1798. In 1820 the original light was replaced with a pair of lighthouses known as "Ma and Pa" or "Mr. and Mrs." Unfortunately, the shorter "Ma" tower was demolished in 1922.

In the late nineteenth century, Bakers Island became home to a fifty-room hotel called the Winne-Eagan, which opened in 1888 and burned completely to the ground from an accidental fire in 1906.

As far as ghost lore, Bakers Island is legendary. For years, the foghorn would sound off without provocation and flickering lights were seen on the island when it was vacant during the off-season. There were also sightings of a horse spirit near the lighthouse. Visitors have reported the smell of hay and disembodied sounds usually associated with four-legged equines like whinnying and hoof stomping.

"Most of the paranormal activity on Bakers Island takes place during the winter months when the island is deserted," wrote Lee Holloway in *Ghosts of the Massachusetts Lights*. "Caretakers have heard what sounds like a party emanating from the Chase Cottage. Workers in the Wells Cottage have been attacked by a 'kissing ghost' and lights are sometimes seen in the general store and Nicholson house when both are closed for the season."

The ghost of Naomi Coyler, who died during a swim off of Bakers Island in the 1960s, is said to haunt the island. There's also a story of a jewel thief who supposedly hid his booty on Bakers. The mysterious flickering orbs are said to be the privateer looking for his buried treasure. In the late 1990s, a group of paranormal investigators reached out to the tightly guarded summer-home community to investigate the so-called evil entity known as the "beast of Bakers Island." However, the paranormal team quickly packed up their belongings and fled once they found out the island doesn't have electricity.

So, what about my encounter with the ghost girl? On the Fourth of July in 1898, a two-level vessel picked up a large group of visitors from Bakers Island and, after dropping off passengers at Salem Willows, tragically capsized en route to Beverly. "The small excursion steamer *Surf City*, with about 60 passengers on board . . . was struck by a sudden, but terrible, squall last evening and capsized," reported the *Fitchburg Sentinel* on July 5, 1898. "The scene, while the work of rescue was going on, was a fearful one, as over half of those on board were women, and their screams could be heard for miles. Many clung to the top of the hurricane deck and supported themselves until the boats came, while others grasped the flag staffs and even the smoke stack."

The majority of the passengers survived the disaster, but eight died, including two teen girls and several unnamed children. My theory is that the ghost girl on Bakers Island is somehow related to the *Surf City* tragedy of 1898.

My stint giving tours on Bakers Island was short-lived. After months of interviews and approvals from the Coast Guard, I only lasted one weekend. I told my boss that the ten-hour workday was too much for me to handle. Truthfully, I was legitimately freaked out by the ghosts still lingering on Bakers Island.

I was moved to the mainland and returned to the city that haunted my dreams for years. Essex Heritage asked me to give their "Myths & Misconceptions" tour in downtown Salem during the summer of 2016. My fingers were crossed that the ghosts from my past would leave me alone.

Bakers Island Light Station is located on Bakers Island in Salem Sound, a sixty-acre island with a large summer colony.

For the most part, they did.

While giving historical-based tours out of Salem's visitor center, I met a few of the characters featured in *Wicked Salem*, including Kathryn Rutkowski, a fellow witch-trials historian who was basically raised at the Rebecca Nurse Homestead in Danvers.

Rutkowski and I would spend afternoons talking about her childhood and what it was like being surrounded by witch-trials history. "When I was younger, the Peabody Essex Museum used to have all of their documents relating to the Salem witch trials out," Rutkowski remembered. "My dad was an electrician there and he would take me on service calls. I would just stare at them and try to read them even though it was so difficult to read. I would look at the artifacts they had, including the archives in Danvers. Seeing something as simple as window glass, it was amazing to think that they looked through that same glass."

In addition to spending weekends exploring the Rebecca Nurse property, Rutkowski would visit the spot behind Danver's Centre Street where it all began, the Reverend Samuel Parris foundation. In 1970 archaeologists excavated the remains of the parsonage house where the afflicted Betty Parris and Abigail Williams first started having fits in January of 1692. "My dad would take me to the Parris foundation and I would look around," she recalled. "It was crazy to think that this was where it all happened."

As far as the initial hysteria involving the nine-year-old Parris girl, Rutkowski said historians should revisit the often overlooked matriarch of the family. "The Reverend Parris's wife, Elizabeth, was always ill and John Indian and Tituba were doing a lot of the work around the house because she was unable to get out of bed," Rutkowski explained. "His daughter Betty had health issues similar to her mom. They both weren't well and what they did back then is if they were ill, they starved them. It was their attempt to remedy an illness, but it just made things worse."

Rutkowski and I had weekly conversations about specifics relating to the witch-trials hysteria. For example, she believed that the ergot poisoning theory is too far-fetched to be true. "Ergotism causes necrotizing symptoms like your fingers or ears will fall off. You would have tremors your entire life," she said. "These people were able to turn on and turn off their afflictions. If it was actual ergotism, they would have symptoms the rest of their lives."

The Essex Heritage manager and creator of the "Myths & Misconceptions" tour insisted that the initial fire that fueled the

Salem witch trials wasn't caused by moldy bread. "The Puritans were not dumb," Rutkowski said. "They knew what ergotism was because they learned about it in England. They knew about the fungus on the plants and knew not to eat it. It's hard to believe that all of what happened in 1692 had to do with rye. It definitely would have affected them long-term."

In 2017 I started to notice a change in the circus atmosphere in Salem, especially in October. The drama that once grabbed headlines transformed from childish "witch war" potshots to grown-up issues that seriously affected the city's future. As a community that seemed forever trapped in the 1980s, Salem was growing up.

In my opinion, Rutkowski is among the new wave of witch-trials historians and her approach is emblematic of the changing climate in Salem. "My hope for the next twenty years is that people can finally just tell what we know as actual fact. When it comes to stuff that's more ambiguous, we should admit that we don't know because we weren't there," Rutkowski continued. "What fascinates people to this day is that it seems like it could be a morbid mystery story. We don't know all of the facts because only parts are written down and it's with a heavily biased tone."

While Rutkowski's "just the facts" approach to Salem's history is literally by the book, she does admit to having a few face-to-face encounters with the ghosts of Salem's past. Of course, this isn't the norm with Salem's older generation, who notoriously keep tight-lipped about the city's hauntings. "My grandmother lived in what they called the Witchcraft Heights area of Salem. She moved from Colby Street, which was part of the Gallows Hill area," she explained. "My uncles always said they saw a woman wearing Puritan garb in the bedroom down in the basement. Both of my uncles described a woman dressed in Puritan garb sitting on their chests and trying to strangle them."

Rutkowski said she had multiple mysterious experiences at her grandmother's historic home in Witchcraft Heights. "When I was a kid, I would go down to the basement and see things that were inexplicable but I just ignored it. I even had imaginary friends," she said with a laugh. "Looking back, I think some of my 'imaginary friends' were real people and I was communicating with ghosts and didn't even know it."

One of her more profound paranormal experiences was near Gallows Hill at the spot historians believe is the execution site. "Years ago I was driving past Proctor's Ledge," she told me. "There was a stop sign and I stopped short because there was a guy in front of my car. I was with my friend and I was like, 'What is this guy doing in front of the street?' And my friend said, 'What guy?'"

Rutkowski said that she then noticed the man was wearing an old-school hood. "I was beeping my horn and my friend thinks I was messing with her. He walked around to her window and looked into the car. He was wearing a seventeenth-century-style hood. It was a cloak. I sped off and then stopped the car to look back. He wasn't there. This happened several years ago before Proctor's Ledge was even talked about. It was terrifying to see this guy pressed up against the window and my friend didn't even see him."

In 2016 a group of scholars confirmed Proctor's Ledge as the location where nineteen innocent people accused of witchcraft were hanged more than three centuries ago. Two years after making the public announcement, the city dedicated a memorial to the victims near the wooded, city-owned area that abuts Proctor and Pope Streets. Officials unveiled the memorial on July 19, 2017, commemorating the anniversary of the hanging of five victims: Rebecca Nurse, Sarah Good, Elizabeth Howe, Susannah Martin, and Sarah Wildes.

One year after the memorial was erected, I decided to revisit the site near a copse of trees after hearing a chilling story from a fellow sensitive, Lynda Williamson Senter. Like Rutkowski, she had a bizarre experience at the execution site located behind the Walgreens on Boston Street. "I had walked to Proctor's Ledge and was taking some pictures while dodging the cars that were coming down the hill," said Senter, adding that she intuitively whipped out her digital recorder and started an impromptu EVP session. "All of

A memorial at Proctor's Ledge honors the twenty innocent victims of the witch trials in Salem, including Sarah Good.

a sudden, everything got really quiet," she said. "The traffic stopped and I recorded for about twenty seconds. On playback, I heard a faint scream along with two words that I couldn't understand."

After spending the day at the Rebecca Nurse Homestead doing some last-minute research for this book and then hearing Senter's story, I felt compelled to visit the confirmed hanging site on my way back to Salem. It was two days after the anniversary of Nurse's execution and it was also Sarah Good's birthday, July 21.

While I was taking photos of the memorial at Proctor's Ledge, a woman holding a bag came up to me and asked, "So, what is this all about? What happened here?"

Her complexion was ruddy, almost as if she was weathered by the sun and the harsh elements of New England. If I had to guess, she was either homeless or a transient carrying all of her belongings in the bag hanging over her shoulder. The woman was young, in her late thirties, but appeared much older.

She reminded me of a modern-day version of Sarah Good. The town beggar woman was thirty-eight when she was hanged at Proctor's Ledge. She was also the first to be interrogated for witchcraft during the trials and, on the day of my visit in July 2018, it was her birthday.

I told the mystery woman that it's Proctor's Ledge, the location where nineteen innocent men and women were hanged for witchcraft more than three hundred years ago. She looked at me, sort of shocked. "I never heard of such a thing," she responded, adding that she's from up north and doesn't know much about the area.

I was taken aback, surprised that she had never heard of the Salem witch trials. Then I asked for her name. "Sarah," she said as

I was pointing to the rocky crevices showing her where the victims were likely dumped into a shallow grave. Beneath my feet was a message carved in stone, "We remember."

I looked behind me to respond to the woman and she was gone. Vanished. Into thin air. And I was shivering in the beauty and the madness of the moment.

Sources

Updated excerpts from my first nine books, including *Ghosts of Salem: Haunts of the Witch City*, *13 Most Haunted Crime Scenes Beyond Boston*, and *Haunted Boston Harbor*, were featured in *Wicked Salem: Exploring Lingering Lore and Legends*. The material in this book is drawn from published sources, including my articles in *DigBoston* and issues of the *New York Times*, *Boston Globe*, *Boston Herald*, *Salem Evening News*, *Salem News*, and North Andover's *Eagle-Tribune*, and television programs like Destination America's *Haunted Towns*, Travel Channel's *Ghost Adventures*, History Channel 2's *Haunted History*, and Syfy's *Ghost Hunters*.

Several books on Salem's paranormal history were used and cited throughout the text. Other New England–based websites and periodicals, like Peter Muise's *New England Folklore* blog, *History of Massachusetts Blog*, and Salem Witch City Ghosts, served as sources. I also conducted firsthand interviews, and some of the material is drawn from my own research. My former Salem-based history tour, "Wicked Salem," hosted at Wicked Good Books, and Essex Heritage's "Myths & Misconceptions" tour were also major sources and generated original content. It should be noted that ghost stories are subjective, and I have made a concerted effort to stick to the historical facts, even if it resulted in debunking an alleged encounter with the paranormal.

Salem, Massachusetts, is famous for its 1692 witch trials, during which several locals were executed for allegedly practicing witchcraft. PHOTO BY SAM BALTRUSIS

Baltrusis, Sam. *Ghosts of Boston: Haunts of the Hub*. Charleston, SC: History Press, 2012.

———. *Ghosts of Salem: Haunts of the Witch City*. Charleston, SC: History Press, 2014.

———. *Haunted Boston Harbor*. Charleston, SC: History Press, 2016.

———. *13 Most Haunted Crime Scenes Beyond Boston*. Boston, MA: Sam Baltrusis, 2016.

Balzano, Christopher. *Haunted Objects: Stories of Ghosts on Your Shelf*. Iola, WI: Krause Publications, 2012.

Boyer, Paul, and Stephen Nissenbaum. *Salem Possessed: The Social Origins of Witchcraft*. Cambridge, MA: Harvard University Press, 1974.

Cahill, Robert Ellis. *Haunted Happenings.* Salem, MA: Old Saltbox Publishing House, 1992.

———. *New England's Ghostly Haunts.* Peabody, MA: Chandler-Smith Publishing House, 1983.

———. *New England's Witches and Wizards.* Peabody, MA: Chandler-Smith Publishing House, 1983.

Calef, Robert. *More Wonders of the Invisible World.* London: Nath. Hillar at the Princess-Arms, 1697.

D'Agostino, Thomas. *A Guide to Haunted New England.* Charleston, SC: History Press, 2009.

Day, Christian. *The Witches' Book of the Dead.* San Francisco, CA: Weiser Books, 2011.

Dowgin, Christopher Jon Luke. *Salem Secret Underground.* Salem, MA: Salem House Press, 2012.

Forest, Christopher. *North Shore Spirits of Massachusetts.* Atglen, PA: Schiffer Publishing, 2003.

Guiley, Rosemary Ellen. *Haunted Salem.* Mechanicsburg, PA: Stackpole Books, 2011.

Hall, Thomas. *Shipwrecks of Massachusetts Bay.* Charleston, SC: History Press, 2012.

Hauk, Dennis William. *Haunted Places: The National Directory.* New York: Penguin Group, 1996.

Hill, Frances. *Hunting for Witches.* Carlisle, MA: Commonwealth Editions, 2002.

Jasper, Mark. *Haunted Inns of New England.* Yarmouthport, MA: On Cape Publications, 2000.

Kampas, Barbara Pero. *The Great Fire of 1914*. Charleston, SC: History Press, 2008.

Macken, Lynda Lee. *Haunted Salem & Beyond*. Forked River, NJ: Black Cat Press, 2001.

Mayhan, Joni. *Dark and Scary Things*. Gardner, MA: Joni Mayhan, 2015.

Muise, Peter. *Legends and Lore of the North Shore*. Charleston, SC: History Press, 2014.

Powers, Edwin. *Crime and Punishment in Early Massachusetts*. Boston, MA: Beacon Press, 1966.

Revai, Cheri. *Haunted Massachusetts: Ghosts and Strange Phenomena of the Bay State*. Mechanicsburg, PA: Stackpole Books, 2005.

Roach, Marilynne. *The Salem Witch Trials: A Day-by-Day Chronicle of a Community Under Siege*. Lanham, MD: Taylor Trade Publishing, 2002.

Rule, Leslie. *When the Ghost Screams: True Stories of Victims Who Haunt*. Kansas City, MO: Andrews McMeel Publishing, 2006.

Saville, Susanne. *Hidden History of Salem*. Charleston, SC: History Press, 2010.

Wilhelm, Robert. *Murder & Mayhem in Essex County*. Charleston, SC: History Press, 2011.

Zwicker, Roxie J. *Haunted Pubs of New England: Raising Spirits of the Past*. Charleston, SC: History Press, 2007.

Acknowledgments

It happened in the middle of Salem's Old Burying Point cemetery on Charter Street. While giving a private tour, I had a moment of clarity. Tala Wolf, a Wiccan high priestess, asked me how *Wicked Salem* is different from my *Ghosts of Salem* book from 2014. While I'm proud of my first exploration of the Witch City, my perspective has changed over the past few years. *Ghosts of Salem* is about haunted locations. *Wicked Salem* is about giving a voice to those without a voice. It's about celebrating Salem's people . . . the good, the bad, and the wicked.

Yes, I had a graveyard epiphany.

The shift in consciousness is from years of hard work, including a season of giving tours at the famed House of the Seven Gables and Essex Heritage, appearing on national TV twice, having hundreds of candid conversations with all sorts of people since unveiling my *Ghosts of Salem* book at Old Town Hall, and reading anything I could get my hands on to make sure that I'm as historically correct as possible.

Since writing my first book, I've developed relationships with the "ghosts" of Salem's past. I also established a bond with Salem's cast of living characters, including local luminaries like Kevin Lynch, Melissa Reynolds, Thomas Vallor O'Brien, Tim Maguire, John Denley, and historians Margo Burns, Kelly Daniell, Gregg Pascoe, and Kathryn Rutkowski. The book also features my friends from the "ghost writer" community, including fellow authors Jack

Kenna, Peter Muise, and Joni Mayhan. Special thanks to Tim Weisberg for recommending me to the *Haunted Towns* crew and penning the book's foreword.

Photographer Frank C. Grace deserves a supernatural slap on the back for capturing the eerie aesthetic of the main haunts featured in this book. I would also like to thank Amy Lyons from Globe Pequot for her support during the process of putting this book together.

There are two women who left an indelible mark on my life (not including my mother, Deborah Hughes Dutcher, or my high-school teacher Beverly Reinschmidt). One is paranormal investigator Lorraine Warren. The other is Laurie Cabot, the "Official Witch" of Salem. Thank you Memie Watson for introducing me to the first lady of witchcraft. I'm truly honored and grateful.

Wicked Salem: Exploring Lingering Lore and Legends is a cautionary tale written with a paranormal lens. This book is about the people—the villains and the victims—who left an indelible psychic imprint at these allegedly haunted locations over a four-hundred-year period.

Wicked Salem is also about correcting the misinformation associated with the witch-trials hysteria of 1692. Over the past decade, I have noticed a shift toward untangling these historical inaccuracies, but we still have a long way to go. Will we ever be completely accurate? No, because we weren't there. However, my goal is to take all of the pieces that we do know and weave together a cohesive narrative that not only educates and entertains my readers but makes the city's "ghosts" proud.

I genuinely care about Salem's people . . . the living and the dead. *Wicked Salem* is for them. I hope I do them justice.

Index

About the Author

Sam Baltrusis, author of the best-selling *Ghosts of Salem: Haunts of the Witch City*, has penned ten historical-based ghost books. He has been featured on several national TV shows including Destination America's *Haunted Towns* and the Travel Channel's *Haunted USA* on Salem and served as Boston's paranormal expert on the Biography Channel's *Haunted Encounters*. Baltrusis moonlights as a tour guide and launched the successful ghost tours "Boston Haunts,"

Doppelgänger? Author Sam Baltrusis specializes in historical haunts and has been featured on several national television shows sharing his experiences with the paranormal.

"Graveyard Getaways," and "Wicked Salem." He also led tours with several heritage organizations including the House of the Seven Gables and Essex Heritage. Baltrusis is a sought-after lecturer who speaks at dozens of paranormal-related events throughout New England, including an author discussion at the Massachusetts State House and a paranormal convention he produced in 2018 called the Plymouth ParaCon. In the past, he has worked for MTV.com, VH1, *Newsweek,* and ABC Radio and as a regional stringer for the *New York Times.* Visit SamBaltrusis.com for more information.